THINK, ACT, BREATHE GLOBAL
And Grow Your Business

By Vernon Darko

Copyright ©2010 by Vernon D. Darko

P.O. Box 890131

Houston, TX 77289

Tel: 281.286.1338. | Fax: 281.286.2825

www.vernondarko.com

ISBN: 978-1-933497-25-9

Printed and bound in the
United States of America

D0868907

TABLE OF CONTENTS

DISCLAIMER

For more information please visit www.vernondarko.com

ABOUT THE AUTHOR

Think, Act, Breathe Global is an innovative book that is relevant and necessary in today's business climate. Many entrepreneurs know that expanding into other countries is a good idea but are unsure of how to go about enacting the practical applications of doing so. There is not a lot of information available via the Internet or through text books which is why this work is so important. What sets apart **Think, Act, Breathe Global** from other sources of information is the personal experience of the author who has successfully put into practice the techniques and strategies found in this book to grow a successful international business. All aspects of going global are compiled in one easy to use book for convenience.

Mr. Vernon D. Darko is President of one of the fastest growing international trading and development companies in the United States. With headquarters in Houston, Texas, and additional satellite offices internationally, EquipXp, LC, under Mr. Darko's leadership, has proven to be a gateway to the world of import and export for companies worldwide. EquipXp, LC in the procurement and global distribution of construction, transportation and heavy lifting equipment, is establishing itself as not only an innovator, but also a leader in the trading industry.

Mr. Darko received his Bachelor of Science degree in Business Administration with an emphasis on International Business, from Lee University in Cleveland, Tennessee. He continued his post-baccalaureate studies at the University of Houston in Houston, Texas, with a concentration in Marketing. In addition to his international background, Mr. Darko managed to heighten his education by presenting a dichotomy of knowledge based on personal as well as professional experiences.

Mr. Darko is a well known international businessman reflected through his current affiliations by presently sitting on the Board of Directors as President, Chairman, and Member, to many prominent organizations such as:

*Educate International Incorporated * EquipXp, LC * ExportImport Bank's SubSaharan Africa Committee * Chief Executive Board, International Organization of CEO's * Restoring Hope International Fellowship Church * Advisory Board, Restoring Hope International Fellowship Church * Board of Governors, Opportunity International Incorporated * Greater Houston Partnership (GHP) * World Trade Committee (GHP) * Africa Committee (GHP)*

Mr. Darko's experience and expertise as Executive Officer, Vice Chairman, Secretary, Treasurer, and Member was also formed by his past associations with organizations such as:

*Board of Directors, International Christian Schools * Board of Directors Trans Atlantic Corp * Trans Atlantic Corporation * Board of Directors, Houston Community Management Services (PCHA) * U.S. Poultry and Egg Association * Food Marketing Institute * Southwest Food Services * CEO Roundtable (GHP) * International Business Issues Committee (GHP) * TEC International Organization of CEOs * Vistage International Organization of CEOs*

Mr. Darko's innovative techniques and experience as well as his dedication to international business make him the ideal person to advise entrepreneurs on how to emerge as a global presence. Helping to enhance others' businesses will also make the world economy stronger as well as more organizations financially lucrative. This is why Mr. Darko has devoted so much time to compiling this book for your benefit.

Mr. Darko states, "One of the questions I have been asked is, 'How did you start your company?' My company is more on the goods and services area. Yes, I've been to school. Yes, I'm educated. Yes, I've learned a lot. But then nothing can teach you more about what you are doing as when you walk through it and go global. It is an experience you have to acquire by working through the process. It is a school of hard knocks as some people would call it. It requires guts just like any company, requires diligence, and requires perseverance."

Mr. Darko has worked through the process. He has guts, diligence and perseverance. In this book he offers his insight to you, so when you decide to go global, you will have a road map of how to accomplish it. It will still take guts, diligence and perseverance to be successful but you will have a tool at your disposal to make the process faster and easier.

Mr. Darko currently resides in Houston, Texas with his wife and four children. In addition to spending time with his family, volunteering at church, and pursuing career and community endeavors, he finds time to engage in extracurricular activities, and maintain physical fitness through his love for golf and basketball. Mr. Darko also enjoys weight training, traveling, reading, and exploring new technology.

INTRODUCTION

Any business can benefit from going global. If you own a United States business and concentrate primarily on customers in the U.S. you are only tapping into a small portion of your potential revenues. However, if you expand into other countries, your potential for success grows exponentially. This may seem like too daunting a task to undertake, though, especially if you are unsure of how to go about breaking into the global market. I know from personal experience that tapping into the global market can be an intimidating experience due to language barriers, differences in culture and other various reasons. However, I am more than confident that this book, Think, Act, Breathe Global will assist you in overcoming some of the foremost apprehensions and hurdles in dealing with foreign markets.

My personal experience in going global will allow you to avoid some of the hurdles I experienced for a streamlined method of breaking into the global marketplace. I wrote this book to allow United States entrepreneurs to take advantage of my wealth of experience and expand their own business for both personal success and to strengthen the overall economy of our great nation. Let the years of knowledge I have attained in this industry help you to grow your business.

Many businesses in the global market remain limited primarily due to a lack of knowledge, ultimately resulting in missed opportunities in foreign countries. This book is designed not only to help you overcome your fears, anxieties and doubts, but enhance your knowledge of global marketing as well. Think, Act, Breathe Global is an excellent tool to increase knowledge and professionalism in the global marketplace. You will obtain the confidence, strength and the strategy to expand your borders and step out of your comfort zone into new and uncharted territories.

This book was written to suggest techniques and to give examples that demonstrate that your business does not have to be limited by remaining local or even national expansion. With strategy, discipline, application and diligence, change in your business will become more and more evident. The techniques outlined in this book will give you the courage to step out and take advantage of not only cross-border commerce, but also the benefits, incentives and the rewards involved for you, your business and the economy of that country resulting in a win-win situation for all.

Think, Act, Breathe Global is a book that appeals to a cornucopia of businesses regardless of size or industry. This book is based on nearly two decades of international market experience and is an excellent reference tool to assist you in conceptualizing and expanding your business into global markets. Although the U.S. population is over 300 million (and yet growing), doing business in the United States is not enough. Think, Act, Breathe Global will teach you:

- *The incentives and benefits of going global*

- *How to take advantage of differences in time zones*

- *How to use various economic situations to your advantage*

- *How to identify quality global clients*

- *How to identify the need in a targeted country*

- *Whether or not your product or service will fill a particular need in a targeted country*

- *How to establish an office in a foreign country*

- *How to establish partners and join forces with larger companies to strengthen your business*

- *How your business can create a win-win situation and boost the economy of that foreign country*

These strategies are just an example of the wealth of knowledge you'll find in this book. You'll obtain practical wisdom and suggestions that will help your business grow from local to national to international. Beyond U.S. borders are 95% of the world's consumers. Within the pages of this book, you have available to you, a solid foundation of intelligence that will enable you to not only go beyond the U.S. borders but to make those consumers your consumers.

If you are reading this then you are likely ready to get to work and start implementing the processes, techniques and strategies found in this book. If you are ready to capitalize on the opportunities available to you by having your product or service reach other countries, then **Think, Act, Breathe Global** will help. There is no time like the present so let's get started!

CHAPTER ONE:

How to Research and Identify a Need in a Foreign Country

In order to catapult your business to the next level, one should take careful consideration into breaking into the international market. Transacting business in the U.S. only is no longer enough! Beyond U.S. borders are 95% of the world's consumers and regardless of the type of business you own or operate, there is not only enough room for the business to flourish and spread beyond local boundaries, but there is a need for your business to expand and reach its untapped territories.

Moving your business into the international market requires a few basic steps, along with a little research. Before taking your first step into the global market, you must understand that there are three types of products1 businesses provide to their consumers and clients. They are:

Goods – Any tangible product that can be sold. Examples of goods that may be sold include automobiles, commodities, clothing, equipment and electronics.

Service – Anything that does not require a tangible item or product. Examples of services include consulting, data processing, legal services, insurance and financial services.

Projects – Involves more assets, methodical planning, engineering, fabrications and organization that are usually long term in nature. Projects combine both goods and services to accomplish a particular broad goal. Examples of projects include building refinery plants, factories, hospitals, hotels and real estate.

A product can be a broad term or a very specific one. For example, I am president of a construction equipment company. Construction equipment is my product. However, within that broad spectrum I have many different specific items. But, your business model may be slightly different where you specialize in a very narrow product. Perhaps you own a winery where all you do is produce wine and you want to export your product to the world. Your product will be the wine which is a much narrower product.

Identify Product to Take Global

Before you can do anything you need to determine what product you want to take to the global market. It is essential that you limit your product to one or two items only. In order to successfully reach a global market you will need to research extensively and become an expert in your product. This is very difficult to do thoroughly if you are spread too thin. Focusing on many different types of goods or services will make you appear to be a novice in the business. You can not do everything. You must be focused on that one particular good or service.

When you attempt to influence others of your competence in several areas, it does not come across very well and it looks unprofessional to your clients, as if you are ineffectual. In addition, your lack of experience in international dealings will soon become evident to all whom you do business with. Such business practices are not beneficial and could result in a subsequent loss of opportunities.

After you have decided on a product and confirmed the demand for the product, then you must find a supplier. Make sure the supplier chosen has and maintains a highly regarded reputation. You want someone who is reliable and trustworthy. You want to work with a company that makes your business their business. But, there will be more discussion on the details of this in later chapters. For now, the important part you should come away with and can not be emphasized enough is focus on one or two products and do not take on more than you should.

When determining what product you want to introduce to the global market, consider your existing business model, your education and your personal experience in the United States. If you already own a business, this can be your product that you take global. For example, if you own a retail store specializing in cookware, the cookware goods would be your product. However, what you do not want to do is diversify to such an extent that you are introducing new products or services to the market before solidifying your current position with your current product.

For example, if you go global with your cookware products you do not want to also introduce a line of garden tools as well. You do not have the experience with this line and you may not come across as an expert in the field, reducing your chances of succeeding in the global marketplace. However, with some research into the specific foreign markets you have a great chance of successfully marketing the cookware product you are already intimately familiar with.

Identify the Foreign Market

The next step is to come up with the countries or areas outside the United States that you feel may benefit from your product. Identify the foreign market you want to go into and which country within that market will benefit from the product type you plan to provide. Once you have an idea of the market you want to enter you will need to research it thoroughly as discussed in the next section of this chapter.

Make sure to keep an open mind about your market, though. You may think a particular market will be lucrative for your product but upon research you may find that the particulars have changed or you may discover a market you never before considered is ripe for your product. In this phase of planning, it is important to be fluid.

Another aspect of researching the foreign market is considering manufacturing your product in one country to sell in another. This allows you to take advantage of reduced overhead costs in a particular country in order to maximize your profits. You can easily choose a country that will allow you to produce your product inexpensively even if that country is not your target consumer for the finished product. More information on this will be discussed in **Chapter Nine: Take Advantage of Trade Financing.**

Necessary Research for Your Product

The final step is to research the specifics of your product as it pertains to your desired market. There are many tools you can use to gather information that will assist you with determining how well your product has the potential to do within that market. You will need to use various available sources to obtain information so you have a complete picture of the potential your product has in the foreign market.

You may use the Internet, library, research books, U.S. Commercial Services[2] and foreign embassies[3]. You may also utilize, for a fee, foreign third party entities to conduct the research for you that will improve time management, save money on overhead costs and help you gain an advantage in the specified market. These companies provide statistics and demographic information that will be invaluable when researching your product in the foreign market. You may even have to travel to the country you've selected to conduct in person research and develop relationships; however, this will be discussed in detail in Chapter Ten.

First, you will need to see if there is a need for your product. You can do this by contacting the commercial services department of the embassy for that country in the U.S. and of the U.S. Embassy in that country[4]. The U.S. Commercial Services is available to you to provide all of the information you need in order to research a particular product, customer, or industry of your choice. They will then inform you of the degree of necessity for that product, customer, or industry. These organizations are able to help walk you through the beginning processes of penetrating the global market. The commercial services department will be able to provide you with a comprehensive list of needs for that country.

Another useful source is the Chamber of Commerce[5] for the country you are interested in. The Chamber should have a world trade division that advertises local merchants, their products and their needs. Lastly, attending trade shows that emphasize global trading, export opportunities and international exploits will give you a first hand look at what the country is in need of.

Look at the overall culture of the country as well as climate and other conditions that may influence the need for your product. For example, are you a furrier? If so, you may find that there is a potential need for your product in cold climates such as Sweden but the odds of the population of Zimbabwe needing a fur coat are slim. Once you've researched and determined that there is a need, then master it!

Another question you will want to ask that is related to whether or not there is a need for the product is whether or not the economy of the country will sustain the cost of your product. For example, in the case of a furrier, even if you reduce manufacturing costs to decrease overhead and are able to reduce the retail cost of the fur coat, this is still a high ticket item.

If you plan on selling this item to a poorer country you will likely find that there is not enough of the population who can afford it to make it worthwhile and profitable. So, make sure you look at the economy of the culture as it pertains to your product. Does the culture support the need for luxury items and does the economy make such an endeavor feasible? Or, are more practical, items the norm at a lesser retail cost? This is a consideration that should be researched before determining if the foreign country is ripe for your product.

Also consider the target consumer within the country. Are you selling primarily to the public sector, private sector or both? Factors that apply to the general population may differ for the government agencies. Even if the private sector business is not enough to sustain a viable profit, if you can make this feasible by selling to the government you can use the private sector as a secondary stream of income. If you do determine the public sector is your target consumer and likely to be the most lucrative, you will then need to research the regulations required to be eligible to deal with government contracts. This, however, will be discussed further in **Chapter Two: Exporting Rules and Regulations.**

Finally, you will need to research the competition within the market. Are there other foreign or domestic suppliers of this particular product within the country? If not, how can you establish your company as the foremost expert in the field? Keep in mind that if you are the first supplier, you will likely not be the last so you will need to consider your business model to deal with future competition.

If there are other suppliers of your product, how can you set yourself apart in order to compete with them? How saturated is the market already? Do you have a plan to reduce costs, improve customer satisfaction, produce a higher quality product or increase product awareness that will give you an advantage over the competition? Is there enough market share left for you to carve out a decent profit?

Research Tools

There are many tools available to you where you can gather data on your product or service. Make sure you exhaust all possibilities so that you have thoroughly researched your product, the market you are trying to break into and the need for that product within the market. Below is a list of some places to start with your research:

• *Local libraries* – There is a wealth of information available at your local library and it is all free. You can collect news stories, statistics, peruse reference materials and check out books and magazines on a particular topic that pertains to your business or the desired foreign market you want to break into.

• *Research books* – If your local library does not have a particular research book, you will likely be able to acquire it through other means such as book stores and Internet auctions. Check some of the book stores such as Barnes and Noble, Borders and Amazon and see if they carry the book or if they can special order it for you.

• *Internet* – With today's technology you can find just about anything you need on the web. This is a highly valuable source of information where you can look through statistics, local websites, government sites and more. Even if you can not obtain all the information you need at a particular website, the website will point you in the right direction to find additional information in person or via other means.

• *U.S. Commercial Services* – The U.S. Commercial Service is the trade promotion unit of the International Trade Administration. They will work with your company to help you get started in exporting or increase your sales to new global markets. Their services include world class market research, trade events that promote your product or service to qualified buyers, introductions to qualified buyers and distributors and counseling and advocacy through every step of the export process.

• *Foreign Embassies* – Foreign embassies located in the United States are great sources of information on local culture as well as specifics on importing and exporting rules.

• *Consulting companies* – These companies specialize in gathering data and statistics for your particular uses. You can find both U.S. based companies that specialize in a particular region or you can search for consulting firms based in the country you are researching.

• *Chamber of Commerce* – Many countries have a Chamber of Commerce that can assist you with research and development of your particular product in that country.

With the list above you should have a good starting point to conduct research. However, this list is by no means exhaustive. See **Chapter Four: Organize a Support Group of Companies** as well as Appendix II for more detailed information regarding resource materials, helpful agencies and supporting companies.

CHAPTER TWO:

Exporting Rules and Regulations

After you have completed the steps in **Chapter One: How to Research and Identify a Need in a Foreign Country,** you will need to research the specific regulations governing export restrictions and requirements to your desired foreign market. There are a few aspects you should be aware of. You need to ensure you are complying with product classifications that are found on the Schedule B, export controls such as licensing requirements and trade party screening to ensure you do not export to an entity that is not allowed. If you violate the regulations for exporting you will be subject to penalties.

Product Classifications

There are two general types of product classifications: Harmonized System (HS) and North American Industry Classification System (NAICS). The Harmonized System is a series of two through ten digit numbers comprising the complete classification of a product. The NAICS system is one that was developed jointly between the United States, Canada and Mexico in order to track trade across North America.

There are over eight thousand commodity classifications in schedule B. If you are looking for your product's classification code, you can go to the U.S. Census Bureau's website and search for your product using their Schedule B database tool[1]. The proper product control classification will help determine licensing requirements as well as whether the product is a controlled substance and subject to particular restrictions.

Export Controls

Some products require licenses in order to export to another country. In such cases, you need to apply for and attain one prior to doing business there. Depending on the product and the destination country there are various items you may need to provide in order to attain the exporting license. There are actually a relatively small number of goods that require licensing but if you are without one and need it you may find yourself burdened with delays and possible penalties. You can determine if your product requires a license by utilizing the Export.gov website[2].

Inspections may be required for various products either before leaving the United States or upon arrival at the destination country. If you are not in possession of the required documentation proving inspection releasing of the product could be delayed or refused, which could result in charging of additional fees and tariffs. In some cases and some countries, there are embargos that do not allow you to ship to the country at all. The SGS North America INC[3], Bureau Veritas Group[4] and Cotecna[5] are all resources you can use to check inspection requirements. These are measures put in place by the foreign government to ensure their citizens don't receive bad products. You can also contact the Chamber of Commerce as well as the embassies in the country you wish to export to.

Possessing the correct documentation for your transaction is just as important as having a passport when traveling to a foreign country. In order to ensure that your paperwork is accurate and complete, I would recommend that you enlist the services of a documentation specialist. There are two primary types of documentation specialists, a freight forwarding company and letters of credit specialist. A freight forwarding company will help determine the shipping method and process all of the shipping documentation needed for your transaction.

If your transaction is not a cash exchange, you will need a ***letter of credit***, referred to as an ***LC***, thus requiring a specialist. A letter of credit specialist will review the financing documentation for your presentation to the bank, to ensure that all the terms and requirements are in compliance with banking guidelines.

Please note, some freight forwarding companies are also trained to review financing documentation as well. Documentation required with letters of credit are commercial invoices, bills of lading, packing lists, certificates of origin, and an inspection report if necessary. If you don't have the correct documentation you run the risk of not getting paid in a timely manner or getting paid at all.

Trade Party Screening

The U.S. Export Administration Regulations (EAR) prohibits trade with specific individuals, companies, institutions and organizations. To remain compliant with export regulations you will need to check the lists to ensure you are not inadvertently doing business with entities that not allowed. Each government department and agency with jurisdiction over exports publishes their own list, which means there are more than 10 lists to check. The Bureau of Industry and Security within the U.S. Department of Commerce is a great place to start your research when considering exporting6.

Penalties for Non Compliance

If you violate U.S. export regulations then you and your company could be fined, banned from future exporting, or even sent to jail. Depending on the severity of the violation, you may be, at best, inconvenienced and at worst face criminal charges. Unfortunately, non compliance with export regulations almost always means both a delay in your goods reaching the desired country and fines that can be exorbitant. However, if you hire a company that specializes in exporting goods, you can avoid these penalties and likely save a lot of money in the process. There are third party shipping and documentation specialists that are well versed in the requirements for your particular product.

Selling to the Government or Public Sector

Often the process of bidding on government contracts or doing business with the local government in a foreign country requires special considerations. You may need to register with the government agency and supply additional documentation in order to be eligible for working with the government. In order to determine if this will apply to your product, contact the Chamber of Commerce within the jurisdiction you wish to export to so you may obtain the requirements for selling your product to the public sector.

www.Export.Gov also has an advocacy program available if you have problems exporting. Advocacy assistance can help you overcome trade barriers, bureaucratic problems, and unfair trading practices and help level the playing field to ensure that your company has the best possible chance to sell its products and service

Researching Regulations

It is important to be very sure that you are in compliance with all rules and regulations governing the exportation of your product to another country. Keep in mind that these regulations may vary according to the type of product as well as the destination country. It is also important to stay current on regulations. As discussed in Chapter Three, there may be changes in regulations due to upheaval or changing political climate. In house tracking of all the regulations required for exporting can often be daunting, time consuming and cost prohibitive.

Plus, if you make even the slightest error you may be subject to delays and fines that will dramatically affect your bottom line. You may even be subjected to criminal prosecution or banning from exporting altogether. This is something you do not want to risk so be sure to research thoroughly. Some of the sources you can turn to include:

• *U.S. Census Bureau* – This site has valuable information on product classifications and can ensure you use the correct coding system to your product. You can then use this system to determine any licensing regulations that are required.

• *Export.Gov* – This site will give information on licensing information that will allow you to determine if your product falls within one of the classifications that require a license. If so, it will give further details on what is needed to obtain one. You can also use this site to file complaints and utilize their advocacy program if you feel you are being treated unfairly.

• *U.S. Department of Commerce* – This site has a list of entities that should be checked before conducting business with them. Restrictions apply as to who you can sell to overseas.

• *Chamber of Commerce* – You may have exporting restrictions or additional information that is needed in order to conduct business with the public sector. Contacting the Chamber of Commerce within the target country will allow you to remain compliant so you are eligible to work with the government.

• *Third Party Documentation Specialists* – This is one of the more common ways to ensure you remain compliant. Because it is their sole job to remain up to date with changing regulations and political climates, you may benefit greatly from utilizing this service. They will ensure all your documents are in order before you ship.

CHAPTER THREE:

Research the Language, Culture and Political Climate

While looking at foreign countries to expand into, it is essential for the business or entrepreneur to research each and every country that is being considered. This research is vital not only for determining whether the selected country is worth further investment of time, energy and capital but also for guaranteeing that the business itself begins on solid footing. The first impression made by a new business in a country can be a recipe for success or disaster depending on how it is approached.

One of the most popular examples of failure due to a lack of research prior to exporting a product that is often cited is the case of the Chevy Nova. When General Motors decided to export the Nova model to Mexico it saw incredibly sluggish sales. It was months later that it was realized that Nova was slang for "no-go."

General Motors could have avoided this completely by doing some research into Mexico's language or even with a twenty minute focus group section with Hispanic immigrants who were living in the United States at the time. Ultimately, they changed the name of the vehicle and saw a great upsweep in sales of that vehicle.

There are four elements of research that the business or entrepreneur needs to do when choosing and isolating countries to do business with. These are language, culture, political climate and financial climate.

Language Research

Language research is vital. While residents are notorious for only speaking one language, many other countries are also famous for strongly preferring one language all the while speaking other languages fluently. This is why the research is so important. The first step, which is fairly easy to do, is to identify the primary and any secondary languages that are used in that country. Understanding which language to use at which time is important.

For example, in Indonesia there are dialects that each island that makes up the country speaks. However, there is a language that has essentially been created that facilitates communication across the country. For business dealings, this main language is absolutely proper and correct. However, if during the process of finding a translator (more on that later) there is one available who knows one or more of the regional dialects, their services will be more productive by dealing with government agencies, prospective local partners and even potential employees in a more personal manner than if that translator simply speaks the national language.

This type of issue is strong in many countries, especially those made of up of different, unique, indigenous peoples all under one umbrella of a government and a national language. Big countries that require this type of research include China, Indonesia, as previously mentioned, as well as Russia and even some of the Middle Eastern countries as well.

By making a point to communicate with any government agencies, using the proper language is also important. While the business community will appreciate the local approach, the government will most likely prefer that the communication be in the primary language. Finding a good translator makes for all the difference in the world though. For those from the United States using this book, the U.S. Commercial Services department1 of the federal government can help find a local translator for many countries.

This department also can provide translating services internally for some specific languages as well, depending on if you are in the initial phases and making phone calls or sending emails or actually going to visit the country. Many of the highly industrialized nations have similar government agencies designed to help facilitate businesses and entrepreneurs in creating exporting outlets. Many of the "first world" nations have huge trade deficits that are only growing larger as more and more goods are produced in China, India and other nations with dramatically lower labor costs.

For emails and other written communications, there are a number of alternate ways of translating without having to involve anyone. Software has come a long way and now can translate effectively; not only getting the words right but also preserving the underlying meaning. There are also translating services available on the Internet, including a few sites that offer basic translation for free. While not perfect, they do fairly well but more focus on the words and grammar rather than the actual words. As you may know, English is a tough language to translate due to words having different meanings and the lack of masculine and feminine words that are integrated into almost every other language on the planet.

The test of any translation software product, whether it is this free translation site: ***http://babelfish.yahoo.com/*** [2] or a pay product is to translate a fairly complex block of text then translate it back. It may not translate into your exact words, but it certainly should convey the exact same meaning. For example, the first two sentences of this paragraph translated from English to German and then back to English looks something like this when using the free site:

"For email and other written reports there are some changing ways of translating, without having to include everyone with. Software came a long way and can now translate effectively; the words quite not only, keep however the which is the basis meaning also, preserving."

While there is some word garble, the sentence is still understandable. However, using the same example but using **Babylon'**, a pay-for software, it yields a bit better results:

"For emails and other written communications, there are a number of alternative ways for the translation without anyone involved. Software has a long way and now translate can effectively; not only the words right, but also preserve the deeper meaning."

For some languages, translation software works very well. For others it can be tedious whether it is free or not. English to Japanese or Chinese, for example, yields very poor results from any translation software. Russian proves to be almost impossible for Babelfish but Babylon does a better job. English to and from Germanic and Latin-based languages is safe, but even moving over to Russia, the translation quality is reduced. Because of this, a human is going to be the better choice for most translation services. Any translation done by a computer needs to be predicated with a disclaimer to the recipient and should further communication be needed, a translator or common language will be necessary to make a business deal work.

Once a county has been selected, there is also the option to learn the language of the country. By learning the language then travelling and using the language, it is a great opportunity to not only master a foreign language; it makes any potential partners or government officials that you are working with in that country really know that you are serious about working in that country. There are two language learning products available that tout excellent results and a wide variety of languages to choose from. While neither of them focus on writing the language, either solution makes the user able to converse in that language; not just merely scrape by to order a meal.

The first and less costly option is ***Transparent Language***[4]. They offer free lessons in a number of languages and have some of the government contracts for training government officials in the language they will need to know for their assigned country. The other is the highly popular and frequently advertised ***Rosetta Stone***[5] software. They too are used by government officials and claim to be the best of the best for teaching people new languages. Neither claims perfection nor reading ability but both claim high success rates, even for those that claim that they cannot learn a new language. The main difference is price with Rosetta Stone being significantly more expensive than Transparent Language.

As you can see, language research is vital and is important to revisit at each phase of establishing an export visit. For the initial phase, knowing what language or languages to use is vital for establishing good contacts in the country. Later on, once a country has been chosen, learning the language that you have researched as being the best language for that country could be the difference between success and failure.

Research the Business Climate, Customs and Values

The second major category of research is into the customs of the countries that you are considering to export to. First of all there is the business climate but also the general customs and values that the country carries. Seemingly small things such as whether to make eye contact or not can make or break a business deal or make a favorable tax situation go sour with a government official. There are many ways to go about understanding the business climate as well as the culture and values of any given country.

Readings on Business Climate

Culture, values and business climate work hand in hand. However, for understanding business climate especially, online research is an excellent start. There are virtual culture centers for many countries, plus **Wikipedia**[6] has become an excellent source of information, typically written and edited by people from the country that is being written about. This research can prove invaluable as a starting point. There may be a country that seems like a great opportunity but turns out, from your research, to be wholly unwelcoming of outside exports and non-residents. Your research has just prevented you from choosing a country that on the surface looked good but would have been a folly to invest in.

Reading on Culture and Values

For understanding cultures, there are many different books available. Because culture is covered in multiple academic fields, it is very easy to get bogged down in wordiness as well as technical jargon specific to the field that the book was intended for. I stumbled across the book *Culture and Organizations: Software of the Mind by Geert Hofstede*[7] a number of years ago and found it both well written and absolutely intriguing. For me, this book struck an excellent balance of technical and non-technical jargon and was written from a business person perspective.

Part of the reason for this is that this book was written about research done by the author for IBM and the book is about his findings based on that research. Essentially, the goal of the book is to not specifically talk about each and every culture in detail but be able to understand a country's culture based on four specific factors. By understanding where a country stands based on those factors, it can help a person properly phrase letters and make sure that the words used pertain to the culture of the country.

For example, one of the measures in **Software of the Mind** is boiled down to individualism versus collectivism. Most cultures are collective in nature; meaning they put groups before the individual. This is true not only for the family unit where multiple generations of people help raise the children but is also true for how business dealings are handled. Asian cultures are especially well known for their business dealings, including things like singling out a worker or workers who built a car that came back to Japan as a lemon.

Their work is not just a job and not really a passion; they are simply there to do their absolute best so the company is successful. Understanding that a culture is more collective in nature will dramatically affect how you will walk into business dealings with that company. Will you work on nurturing a relationship with the company or simply walk in with a business appropriate coolness? Your cultural research will help you know which way is appropriate for the country.

Talk to People

There are many avenues to talking to people about a country's business climate, culture and values. First of all, the embassy for that nation is an excellent place to start. One of the functions of an embassy is to help those who wish to open businesses have a place to get basic information to do so. An embassy is full of people from that country and can clue you into not only that country's business climate but also foreign trade laws and even current likes and dislikes of the people of that country. It can be an excellent but general starting point.

Another way of going about getting good quality information about a country is to speak with someone who is a business person who used to live in that country. Placing an advertisement in the paper, using an online classifieds such as ***Craigslist*** or simply through networking with your contacts, friends and peers should result in finding someone willing to talk to you; or at the very least willing to sit down with you for an hour for a small amount of money.

Getting face time with someone can get you some of the best information you can get, especially if they are business and entrepreneur oriented themselves. For example, the embassy may tell you a glossed-over version of the business climate of a country, where the person who has emigrated will more than likely have a starker viewpoint. By taking both perspectives with some caution, you can merge the two into the most realistic version of the country's true outlook.

When you have settled on a country or countries that you intend to export to, finding business partners who frequently travel back to the area or are interested in doing so can be invaluable. *(Chapter 5 covers this in detail.)* Some of those who you spoke to and interviewed may end up becoming candidates for and eventually business partners for your export venture into a specific country. If they appear to have potential as a partner, it is important to screen them with the U.S. Commercial Services department, or your country's equivalent, to be sure they are reputable before going into business with them. Remember, always think ahead when you are preparing. The initial research that was done to pick countries to export to can yield important contacts and help your later leg work if you keep yourself organized and forward thinking throughout the process.

Political Climate

Research into the political climate of any countries you are considering exporting to is incredibly important. A few years back, a number of international oil companies were hit and hit hard because of a change in politics in Venezuela. Once Hugo Chavez had attained power, the country became more and more of a communist economy and government and one day the country essentially seized and nationalized the entire oil industry.

All of the equipment that was in the country suddenly belonged to the government and all of the capital invested in the country's oil infrastructure was gone at that point. While this is extreme, even a small export business could find themselves completely stuck should a country's political climate be volatile or appear that it is on the road to being volatile. By researching, you can avoid countries that look to be on the path to destabilization. There are five elements of the political climate that must be addressed and researched before going into business in a country:

1. Is The Country At War?

While a country that is at war may seem like a country to avoid completely, it could actually be a good investment. For many countries, there are tribal wars going on in outlying areas but the core of the country is safe. Religious wars tend to also be more isolated to particular regions of a country. For both tribal and religious-based conflicts, there could still be an opportunity for investment in exports for areas that are considered neutral or safe zones. There is more risk for any country that is at war for both you and any business associates you find that live in the country but there will also be more opportunity because fewer companies will be willing to invest.

2.   Is the Country you are Researching a Communist Country?

As with the example given in the introduction to this section, communist countries are far more likely to change the rules at any point when it comes to ventures of a capitalist nature. While they may welcome you and your goods with open arms, getting money out of the country could be more difficult or on unfavorable terms or they could simply decide to seize your business. On top of this, the income of the typical citizen of a communist country is typically not going to allow the citizens to have much money to spend on luxuries.

Because of these issues, think hard before investing in exporting to a communist country. Exxon and Shell oil companies were able to easily survive when Venezuela nationalized their entire oil business because they are massive international corporations. If your small business has invested half of your export business in a country that suddenly changes the rules in a manner that shuts down your business in that country, will the other half of your business be enough to keep it afloat?

3.   How Safe Is the Country?

While a country may not be at war, the safety and security of you while you are visiting as well as any employees you happen to have in the country is paramount to deciding whether you really want to do business in that country. Some countries are notorious for the lack of safety, especially the safety of foreigners. For some countries, the country of origin of the person can equate to how safe they will be in some countries. For U.S. citizens, even a trip to Mexico these days can be incredibly unsafe, with the murder and kidnap rates of foreign nationals becoming more and more prevalent.

Some companies isolate their employees to prevent them from being the subject of violence while in specific countries that are violence prone and will pay for private security forces in those countries. An employee who recently stopped working for a drilling services firm in Angola told me that he would land in Angola on a chartered flight and would be escorted by armed guard to the helicopter pad that was located on the coastline to be flown to the offshore rig that he worked on. For the couple of trips over that he did not fly right out to a rig, he would be escorted to the staff house that had armed guards twenty-four hours a day and any shopping or other in town ventures were accompanied by an armed driver.

For your upstart venture, this may neither be feasible nor profitable so noting such things is important while choosing countries to export to. The website *Nationmaster.com* has an excellent selection of resources, including crime statistics graphs for murder, kidnappings and other types of crime. Doing some research on this site, as well as speaking to your country's embassy that is in that country are both excellent resources for determining the safety of that country for an average person.

4. Research To Do If The Country Is In Distress

When a country is in distress, some of the rules change for importing goods into the country. Rather than trying to invest wholly into the country itself, it becomes far more advantageous to partner with a company that already has established itself in that country. By partnering with them, you may be losing out on a portion of your revenue but are also mitigating quite a bit of risk by utilizing their contacts, their established exporting and importing channels into the country as well as any security that has been established by that company within the distressed country.

Part of your research, if you find a product or service that a distressed country needs, is finding companies already doing business in that country and begin to build relationships with representatives of those companies so you can piggyback your way into the country with their assistance.

5. Considerations When A Country Is In Distress

Finally, when considering a country that is in distress, you must realize that there is more risk involved. Whether it is political unrest, religious tension, inflation or something like famine or drought a country that is in any kind of distress is far more likely to take drastic measures than a country that is stable. You have to be aware that if you establish a business in a distressed country, that it could suddenly become a losing venture.

Imagine the many western businesses that were once open in Iran that are now subject not only to internal struggles from Iran but are also subject to embargos of that country from much of the rest of the world. If you have a product to sell there, the money from that product cannot be sent back to you and no new product can be imported to the country. To emphasize, distressed countries may have better rewards but the risks can be much higher as well. The key is to diversify the countries you export to and to be certain that any investments in distressed countries can be compensated for should a worst-case scenario happen in one or more of those countries.

Ability to Conduct Financial Transactions

The final element of country-specific research that needs to be done and is vital is research on conducting financial transactions in the countries that you are considering building a business in. It does no good to be successful in a country but be unable to get the profits back to you in your country. Some countries still have artificially high exchange rates as well and diligence on your part is needed to see if there is an equitable exchange rate for outgoing money versus incoming money.

While these countries are not as common as they once were, some still require that you exchange all of your money through them; preventing their money from leaving the country and forcing you to accept the different, less favorable, exchange rate before wiring money or taking money out of the country. The four elements of research that you must do revolving around financial issues are as follows:

1. Can You Wire Money Out of the Country?

Wiring money out of the country may not be the cheapest method of transferring money from one country's banks to another but it is efficient; not to mention secure and quick. However, either the country that you are researching or your home country may not allow this type of transaction to occur. For United States residents, the United States Treasury has an **Office of Foreign Assets Control**[9] that regulates and enforced monetary transfers from country to country. Some quick research here can show you if the country or countries you are considering are on a regulated list and what types of regulations are there for that country. Some research into the countries you are considering will be necessary as well to see if that country allows wiring of funds and whether those funds can be sent in their currency or if they must be converted first before being wired.

2.   Do the Banks have Sufficient Foreign Currency to Trade?

You will want to try to find out if the local banks in that country have proper support for doing currency exchanges. This will require diligence, not to mention a translator to speak to banking representatives in the nations you are looking into. Having sufficient foreign currency is vital to keeping your business in and out of the country going. Even if you are wiring funds, the need for the bank to have sufficient foreign currency is essential to keeping foreign businesses going.

To check this, there are multiple avenues. Embassies tend to have this type of information as well as the central bank of the country. This may require an international phone call and a translator as many countries do not publish this information on the Internet. There are also third party companies that rate banks from across the globe. Essentially credit reporting agencies for banks, these sites provide useful information. Of these, **Moodys.com**[10] offers excellent information but is a subscription service. **Fitchratings.com**[11] offers many different reports but these cost quite a bit of money for each report. Finally BankScope.com[12] offers detailed analysis as well as a free trial offer, which would be immensely useful for the person doing research on only a couple countries.

3.   Are the Country's Banks Reputable?

While most countries regulate their banking industries heavily, there are many countries that let the banks have a lot more freedom than others. Some of these countries have banking systems that take advantage of that freedom in ways that are unethical and oftentimes illegal in most other countries. Because of this, there are ways of going about finding out if a country's banking system is on the up and up. The **International Finance Corporation** or **IFC** is a division of the **World Bank.** Currently, 182 countries are members of the IFC and all countries that are members must have banking regulations established that abide by the IFC's **ARTICLES OF AGREEMENT.**[13] If the country you are looking into exporting to is a member of the IFC, they are going to have a reputable banking industry. Other research through your country's presence in that country can also help ascertain whether the country has reputable banking as well.

4.   Are you able to move 100% of your profits out of the country or must some stay in the country?

Many countries restrict how much profit a company or entrepreneur can take out of the country once it has been earned. This helps keep money in the country as well as encourages investment and growth within the country. While most countries have some limits on this, most realize that limiting the profits of outside companies too much will prevent growth and investment in the country. This can be researched through a variety of channels, including web searches of individual country's policies, Wikipedia as well as calls, letters or emails to local embassy's for the countries you are researching.

CHAPTER FOUR:

Organize a Support Group of Companies

Most successful businesses have a group of supporting businesses that assist them with their daily operations. The services your company requires may include legal, financial, marketing, shipping and others.

This is no different in a foreign country and you may very well need experts who know the ins and outs of dealing with a particular country's regulations and customs. Keep in mind that you can find both U.S. based as well as local companies to conduct business with and in some cases you may need to develop partnerships both in the U.S. as well as abroad.

This is why it is very important to establish and maintain a solid working relationship with your supporting companies. You should consider these companies your partners and treat them well. Make sure you are always ethical in your dealings and expect the same in return. Some support companies you may need to use include:

Manufacturer or Vendor

Maintaining a good relationship with your manufacturer or vendor of your product could mean the difference between making a sale and losing a sale. Make sure the vendors are capable of handling the volume your business will produce or have resources available to accommodate. Also, look toward future growth. Your manufacturer may be able to keep up with your current demand but will they be able to continue to deliver quality materials on time if your business expands?

Your manufacturer or vendor will greatly influence many facets of your business. The quality of your product, how quickly it is turned around and quantity expectations all rely on the manufacturer or vendor so it is imperative to research this thoroughly. The Internet, embassies, Chamber of Commerce and the U.S. Commercial Services are all great sources of information to start looking.

There are several considerations for determining your manufacturer but one of the most important is whether or not to manufacture in the United States or abroad. Often manufacturing in the United States is much more expensive. However, you also have some advantages as far as quality and production are concerned. There is also a sense of national pride that may come into play and if the cost differences are negligible you may opt for a U.S. manufacturer.

There may also be difficulties when it comes to intellectual property that you may want to consider before choosing a foreign manufacturer over a U.S. one. If the country you are considering has a reputation of stealing the intellectual property of the manufacturer you may want to reconsider. China, for example, is a prime example of this and although production costs are lower, the theft of your intellectual property may not be worth it. If this is not a concern, though, look to the bottom line. The trick is to find the correct balance that will give you quality at an appropriate cost.1

When researching vendors, you should not be dissuaded from approaching a vendor that does retail sales or even one that does their own exporting either. Most companies, at best, will have an incredibly limited export department consisting typically of only two or three people. For most companies, their export department is only responsible for twenty percent of their revenue and exporting and importing is an often overlooked and underutilized area of the company's business plan.

Because of this, they have little time or other resources to devote to doing the legwork needed to expand their exports to new places or even to properly export to their existing ones. Your goal is to increase the activity in the export market and if you can take over and improve on a vendor's exporting ventures it increases their sales with very little work on the vendor's part.

Transportation and Shipping

Transportation and shipping is your lifeline to your customers. If you fail to deliver your product when you say you will it will affect you and future business for your export business, even if it is out of your hands and was caused by the shipping company. You will want to make sure that the company you deal with has a fleet of vessels that will suit your needs and is also experienced with transporting cargo from one country to another.

It should be noted that there is a distinction between transportation, shipping and export/import companies. While some of their duties overlap, they are distinct entities with different business models. Depending on how you are proceeding with your business plan, you may need to either utilize only one of these services or move from one to another as your business grows.

Shipping

For any business looking to start exporting, Shipping services are going to be your first line of assistance with getting your product into customer's hands. While building your business, they will be the ones taking packages from you in your home country and getting them to the customer. They will not be the most cost efficient method of getting your product from point A to point B but should be reliable and relatively quick. Even if you are building your business, you will still be utilizing a shipping company of some sort to move your product from your office or warehouse within the country to the customer.

Shipping companies focus on full-service point A to point B transport of goods and charge accordingly. They handle everything, including duties, import taxes and the like for the goods that you are shipping.

However, they are expensive and you will want to try to move on from utilizing international shipping quickly to increase profit as well as to garner more sales.

Export/Import Company

A company that specializes in export and imports is going to be able to help get larger quantities of your product into the country you want to export to. They work on your behalf for clearing customs in the destination country and will typically handle the transportation of those goods to the country and into a place of your choosing. From there, your local agent will receive the goods and begin shipping them out to customers from within the country; drastically reducing the shipping costs of the item.

Transportation Services

Transportations services are the lowest cost option for getting your goods from port to port; however, they are not the quickest most of the time. With a transportation service, you or your overseas agent will be responsible for handling the customs side of things on the receiving side. You will likely be dealing with larger quantities of goods as well and will be shipping them from the manufacturer to the agent directly and it will be by ship.

Because of this, the time for the goods to get to the destination country is quite a bit longer but the cost per item is far cheaper, especially for larger items. Once your business is going well or if you are investing quite a bit initially to get your business presence in a country and you have access to someone in the country that specializes in customs for the country, it makes for good business sense to utilize a transportation company to get your goods to the country.

Research

For any company that you want to use to get your product to your destination country, you must do some research on the company to make sure they are a legit and reliable company to do business with.2 For those in the United States, the BBB, or Better Business Bureau is an excellent place to begin3. They are an independent agency that investigates consumer complaints and strives to be non-biased with their investigation of those complaints. This agency has similar agencies for Europe and Asia as well and is a great starting place for any research into the reliability of a company of any sort but especially those that deal directly with single individuals and small businesses.

Another method of research is to check ratings, testimonials and even get references from the company or companies you are considering to use. There are many third party websites that rate companies that can be used as a method of investigation. Testimonials are a great place to start as well but must be taken with a grain of salt. Would any company want to publish negative feedback about themselves?

Again, third party sites are your best opportunity to get honest feedback about the company. Another option is to request and contact references. Ask them questions about the service and timeliness of the company as well as how they have handled any issues that have come up. Between these investigative tools you will find a company that fits your needs at a fair price point.

Freight Forwarding Company

Freight forwarding companies are an interesting combination of some of the above mentioned transportation and shipping solutions.4 A freight forwarding company takes your goods and helps get them to their destination just like a shipping company but are more focused on small companies. They will prepare the documents for you, the exporter and essentially serve as the middleman between you, the transporting company to get the goods to the destination company and the shipping company in the destination company.

They will have contracts with both the transportation and shipping companies that in most cases will get you lower rates. By working with multiple companies on the export side, for instance, they can ensure that a shipping container is completely full. They buy the cargo space for the shipping container and fill it with the goods from multiple companies and small vendors that otherwise would have to pay for an entire container even though they only needed a fraction of the room inside.

Insurance Company

Getting insurance for a business venture is vital and having an insurance agent that you can rely on and trust to handle your insurance needs is even more important. A personal relationship here can go a long way to making sure you are always properly covered as well as getting the best rate at all times. There are two primary forms of insurance that you absolutely must have. These are both vital to you and your business venture.

Insurance of the Product

Your goods are your livelihood and should they go missing you need to be covered. Often, this type of insurance is built into your shipping or is something that is offered as an option. If you utilize a freight forwarding company, they will likely have a contract with an insurance company for this type of insurance. Should your goods be damaged, stolen or destroyed during shipping, you will receive a payment from the insurance company. This may cover your costs or your costs plus what you would have paid had they all sold at retail price. It depends on the insurance and how much you are willing to pay.

A couple years ago, a freighter listed heavily and a large number of cars made by Audi ended up sliding into the ocean and sinking to the bottom. They were obviously ruined. However, Audi over-insures their vehicles because they have such a spotless claim record as well as getting better rates because of how much they ship. They ended up making a larger profit off the vehicles on the bottom of the ocean than those that they sell at the dealership because of their foresight.

Financing Insurance

The second type of insurance that any exporter should carry is insurance to insure the financing. Even if on your end you are essentially paying cash for the goods, it is possible to be covered should the goods or your company in the destination country be seized or otherwise taken over because of political reasons or unrest. Loss of business insurance and financing insurance are both types of insurance that should be looked into when investing in another country.

Business Insurance

There are other forms of business insurance that may be considered as well though are not as mandatory. Included in this are forms of insurance such as liability insurance which insulates you from claims should the product be defective and cause the customer harm as well as business insurance and property insurance should you open an office in the country you are exporting to.

Documentation Specialist Company

A document specialist company is an entity that processes all sensitive documents relating to the shipment of your product. They are responsible for keeping the documents accessible at all times by both the exporter and the banks. They ensure that documents are in correct order to present to the buyer and financial institutions. A document specialist company is not required in order to export but it can be very convenient.

This is especially true if you are just starting out or have very little experience with exporting regulations. The document specialist will ensure there are no fines levied against you for non compliance and they will also ensure that there are no delays in shipment due to paperwork being incomplete or filled out incorrectly. Some of the documents a document specialist may handle include:5

> *Letters of credit*
> *Forwarding documents*
> *Airway bill*
> *Bill of lading*
> *Commercial invoice*
> *Packing list*
> *EEI (Electronic Export Information) form*
> *Certificate of Origin*
> *Licenses*
> *Product specific requirements*

Translation Services

When dealing with a foreign country that also speaks English the use of a translator is not necessary. However, if the primary language of the country you are dealing with is not English you may need the assistance of a translation service. Conducting business in the language of your target country is highly valuable and will typically allow you to increase profits. This illustrates to the entities you are dealing with that you are sensitive to the culture of the country and this will add a sense of professionalism to your company and confidence in your company from others.

Translation services are necessary for both written and verbal communication. Written communication can include email correspondence, online customer support, legal and contractual documentation, advertisements and web sites. If you have all written documentation and correspondence available in the native language then the companies you work with will feel more confident and trust you more.

Verbal communication is also important and use of a translator for meetings is essential to gain a sense of professionalism with executives from a foreign country. Utilizing their native language will instill a sense of confidence and respect that will assist you in building a solid relationship. When traveling to the foreign country having a translator on hand will be greatly beneficial. However, other verbal communication such as customer service phone calls you should consider to hire native language speakers.

Real Estate

You may not always need the services of a real estate professional but if you are setting up a business in a foreign land there are benefits to establishing a business. If you are frequently traveling to the country you may also consider purchasing or renting a residence. A real estate professional within the destination country will help you search for the best possible real estate for your needs at the best possible prices.

You will also be able to benefit from the expertise of a local real estate agent. They will be able to assist you with the best positioning of an office in a particular area. They will also be able to give you valuable zoning information and pricing. Using a local real estate agent will assist you in finding exactly the property you need for your budget for both residential and commercial properties.

Financial

There are many aspects to your financial needs. You may want consider your local needs as well as your base company needs. Finding a United States partner for your financial needs will ensure the big picture of the company is looked after and ensuring you retain a U.S. company with expertise in foreign trading is essential. However, it is often also beneficial to establish local relationships for your specific financial needs within the foreign country.

Banking

It is important to establish a relationship with a U.S. bank capable of handling complex international transactions. Your local credit union in the U.S. may be able to give you benefit of lower costs of business but if they have no international experience it may be inconvenient for you at best or even cost you money in the long run. It is also beneficial for local transactions to establish a local banking relationship.

Similarly to your U.S. counterpart, you will want a bank in the foreign country that is familiar with transactions between that country and the United States.

Tax Preparation

You will need to pay taxes in the United States based on your revenue. Some tax preparation can be rather complicated when dealing with exports so it is important to find an accountant or accounting firm that is familiar with the complexities of international trade. There will likely also be taxes and tariffs that are required to be paid on the local level. Unless your U.S. firm is well versed with the taxing requirements of the country it may benefit you to have a specialist available to you within the country.

If your local tax agent has experience working internationally, this will be even more beneficial. You can maintain a relationship with both entities and they can work together to ensure you are paying everything you are required to as well as that you are taking advantage of as many breaks as you possibly can.

Financial Reporting

Keeping your books is very important to process improvement. If you do not know how profitable you are, where you are taking in money and where money is going out, you will not know how to improve your business. A local bookkeeping firm or local accounting specialist will be able to keep your books and deal with money transfers. You can track all local overhead expenses and communicate with other financial entities with a local company.

Legal

There are many aspects to legal services you may need. You may need contracts drawn up or advice on regulatory practices. There are many law firms specializing in international law based in the United States. They may also recommend utilizing the services of a local law firm to assist and coordinate from the destination country. Language is one benefit if using a local company. Most international law firms will be able to assist you in finding a local agency if one is necessary.

Advertising

There are multiple forms of advertising you may want to consider when dealing with foreign trade. Of course, the Internet connects everyone worldwide and it is highly beneficial to have a web presence that allows access to your product from multiple countries. But there is also an advantage to doing offline advertising such as print and media ads in the local country and for that a local agency may be beneficial.

Online Advertising

Online advertising comes in many forms. At its most basic, there are sites that allow users to post the equivalent of online classified ads. In the past few years, the popularity of the site Craigslist.org has grown significantly.6 The original site was created in 1995 and really was around at the birth of the internet becoming mainstream and accessible to people in many countries.

Today, craigslist boasts fifty million new advertisements per month. Currently, Craigslist.org is available in five languages, and is the seventh most frequented English language site in the world. There are listings on craigslist.org for sixty different countries around the world. For the person who is looking to export into one of the markets that craigslist offers advertising in, it is a great place to start with their online advertising.

From here, online advertising gets a little more complex and entire books have been written on the topic of maximizing online advertising for any type of advertising campaign. For most types of online advertising, you will need to create a website or portal to what you are offering for sale in the export market you are working in.

Getting web space is easy through many different sites as is registering domains for around the globe. Developing good web content can be done through a third party coder or a basic page can be created easily in Microsoft Word and expanded upon later as your venture becomes more profitable. Chances are, someone you are working with will know someone who does web coding and if you were to hire a full service advertising firm they would offer web development as part of the package.

Each of the major web search companies offers advertising plans. For Google, they call the plan AdWords. When you setup an AdWords campaign, you can specify the country, region or even city to focus your campaign around. When someone does a search for a specified search term, the ad or link to your site will come up. You would pick the search terms when building the AdWords campaign.

For instance, your Widget is something that many people in Bolivia may want but no one sells them directly in the country. If you build your web page around the Widget and the fact that you are selling them without any type of huge markup or international shipping rates then create the AdWords campaign around Bolivians typing in the search term Widget, the column on the right, as well as the advertising supported results will be some of the first ones they see.

On top of this, you will likely, after a while, have your actual web site begin to show up as part of the search results as well as the advertisement portion. There will be third party websites as well that use the flipside of AdWords called AdSense to generate money from AdWords users. If someone does an article about things related to your Widgets or a number of other related words and has AdSense in place, your ad will be seen on their site as well.

For this type of campaign, finding an advertising firm that specializes in this type of advertising will be one way to maximize your time. If you are the type of person to try to do as much as you can on your own, this really is something that can be done easily. There are a number of books available on the topic, from "dummies" series books available at bookstores to eBooks that vary in cost from less than twenty dollars to over one hundred.

Offline Advertising

Offline advertising still needs to be an integral part of your advertising strategy. Many of the countries you are targeting, while advanced, are not nearly as connected to the Internet as people are in the "western" world. Print media, especially, is still quite a bit more in favor in a lot of the world compared to how the papers in the United States and Europe are currently fairing.

Because of this, finding an advertising agency that works in the country or countries you are intending to export to is vital. They should be able to create print and other offline advertising campaigns for you and be willing to work with you on different advertisement mediums in the country.

Depending on the scope of what you are exporting, it will determine what offline advertising forms you will rely on to get your product out into the market. You could be beginning with a simple classified ad in the national paper or hitting the TV and radio airwaves for the country with a professional quality advertisement – it all depends on your product, the expected response, the inventory you will have when the campaign begins, not to mention your budget.

Administrative Agencies

Outsourcing administrative duties is becoming more and more popular and this is no different when you set up a company in a foreign country you are exporting to a foreign country. You may want to consider administrative support services outsourcing for secretarial and receptionist needs. Often the cost of this is much less expensive than hiring a full time employee. You can even contact an administrative agency to find a group or person who speaks the language of the country you are exporting to. In the case of multiple countries, some administrative agencies recruit employees who speak various languages to accommodate these needs.

Bookkeeping services are another aspect of administrative work that you may consider outsourcing. This is especially true if you do not have extensive daily work that justifies a full time employee. You can have an agency take care of the bookkeeping on a part time basis and get charged only for the time you utilize the service or by the project.

Payroll services are likely the most often outsourced function of a company. There are payroll services that can handle all your needs. They can create payroll checks for employees all over the U.S. and the world, abiding by the proper laws of the area. They can even accommodate benefits and bonus structures as well as different taxing requirements for the areas. At the end of the year or more frequently if needed, they will prepare the necessary documentation to go to the employees as well as to your accounting professional for business tax purposes.

Employment Agencies

Employment agencies provide a valuable service for human resources. If you need staffing on either a permanent or temporary basis, having a relationship with an employment agency will be highly beneficial. You can use them to hire for open positions when initially staffing your office or when expanding. You can also use them for temporary assistance when you have an employee on extended leave or if you have a rush or special project requiring additional, part time, temporary help.

Staffing your Office

If you are based in the United States it may be necessary to hire employees who are familiar with the culture of the foreign country or who may even know the language. This can be a difficult and time consuming task. However, if you develop a relationship with an employment agency, head hunter or recruiting firm you can save a lot of time searching for ideal candidates.

The same holds true if you are establishing a local office and need employees to staff your office. You can work with a local employment agency to find quality personnel in your salary range who are qualified to do the job. This will save a lot of money and time in your recruiting process because you will already know your candidates are pre qualified.

What you will do with an employment agency is work with them closely to communicate your needs. You will give them a job description, skills needed, education needed and any language requirements you may need. You will also give them a salary range to work within.

The employment agency will do all the leg work. They will advertise for the position and gather resumes. They will screen applicants' resumes and eliminate those who do not qualify. From there, they will do pre interview screening. They may conduct tests to ensure all the qualifications are met and will likely do background checks and reference checks. This way you are sure to get properly vetted candidates.

Once this process is complete you will receive a list of the candidates who qualify along with their resume. You can then work it one of two ways. You can conduct interviews with the candidates, narrow down to your chosen applicant and hire them. Or, you can contract with the employment agency and have the best candidate work as a temporary position for a trial period.

This way you can see if they will work out for you without investing a lot of money or any of the financial responsibility for their payroll. You pay the employment agency an hourly rate instead. If the candidate works out you can choose to hire them on as permanent staff whenever you wish.

Temporary Assistance

Perhaps you have a very important client who gives you a rush job. This is above and beyond your typical work load and in order to fulfill it you will need a few extra workers to accommodate the increase in work load. You do not want to hire someone permanently and then have no use for them. The answer is temporary assistance.

Seasonal help may also be needed. If you have a business that booms at a particular time you may need some temporary help for just that period of time. Businesses that specialize in holiday products are especially prone to this but any type of business may see an increase in demand during a particular season. In order to fulfill the demand you may need additional assistance. However, you will not need this when business goes back to normal.

Another reason you may need temporary help is if you have a permanent employee who is out for medical or personal reasons. This is especially true if on extended leave such as for maternity. That person still has a job to do and a role to fulfill and you will need someone to fill in for the time being. An employment agency familiar with your needs can draw from a pool of qualified personnel to accommodate your temporary or part time needs.

Communication Service Provider

Communication is key when it comes to going global and it is essential that you choose communication service providers that will accommodate your needs. You will need telephone, mobile and Internet services to properly service your customers and to conduct business.

Telephone – You need to have a telephone company in order to speak with your customers and vendors. You will either need to find a local company that can give you quality service in your local office or a U.S. based company that will give you good deals on international calls. You may also need a toll free number, international toll free number or multiple line functionality. Make sure to shop around to get the best blend of quality, service and price. The telephone is also related to faxes which will also be necessary.

Mobile Services – You will need a service provider to support mobile services for your cell phone, laptop or PDA. When in the U.S. you need inexpensive rates for when you have to use your cell phone to contact offices or people in the foreign country. Make sure you choose a plan that gives you the most for your money and has a solid network in the country you need to call the most so you have no disruption in service. When travelling you also need to consider your usage and any roaming fees that are applied. Contact your service provider to see how they can accommodate your travel. A good mobile provider will typically also have the necessary facilities to accommodate your data usage needs for a PDA or laptop computer.

Internet Services – Whether in the United States or in the foreign country you will have to have access to the Internet. You will need a web presence to be hosted either in the foreign country or in the U.S. home office. Consider both reliability and price. You will also need access from your office to the Internet. If you have an established office in the foreign country, all your work stations will need Internet access so ensure you have speed, reliability and a reasonable price.

Key Points to Remember

Establishing a support group of companies is essential in successfully running your business. However, there are also some key points to remember when establishing and maintaining these relationships:

You are trading in a global market which is much larger than the U.S. market.

Having a strong support network will enhance your capabilities, presentation, timeliness to respond and overall performance when transacting business.

Make sure you take care of your support team so they will take care of you:
- *Respond to their needs*
- *Pay their invoices on time*
- *Operate within ethical boundaries*
- *Keep open lines of communication*

I strongly believe that you reap what you sow, therefore, do unto others as you would have them do unto you. These supporting companies will help your business grow and thrive. But you need to do the right thing by them. Establish strong relationships and maintain them. If you treat your supporting companies right, pay on time, communicate effectively and do not make unreasonable or unethical demands, they will go the extra mile for you.

Keeping a group of supporting companies and maintaining a positive relationship with them can mean the difference between being successful in business and struggling or even failing. For more information on the importance of relationships, see Chapter Thirteen: Establishing and Maintaining Relationships.

CHAPTER FIVE:

Find a Foreign Partner or Agent

In your travels as well as your research to build your exporting business, you are going to come across people who could potentially become your foreign partner or agent. Finding someone to serve as your local contact for a business is incredibly important to the success of your exporting business.

The person you choose is going to be responsible to do most of the ground work in terms of developing the business in your chosen country as well as developing relationships with other businesses and helping get past any government red tape involved in the creation and maintenance of your business venture in that country.

There are two critical elements to finding someone to be your foreign partner or agent. First off is simply finding a group of candidates. The second element is checking their background to make sure they are legitimate and trustworthy business partners.

Building a Pool of Candidates

Building a pool of potential partners is a great start to finding the right one for you. Some of this may have happened while researching the culture and business practices of the country or countries you were researching. On top of any potential business partners this research yielded other places to find agents and business partners include:

1.   ***Conferences that promote foreign trade*** – This is a great place to start as a way to network especially. Once you have narrowed down the countries that you intend to try to export to attending these conferences gets your name out there and gives you a chance to find business people who focus on the regions that you are looking at exporting to. Building contacts here can help you start building your pool of candidates to work with later.

2.   *Networking and Business Referrals from your travels* –
Everywhere you go, talk about your business because you never know
who might be listening. For instance if you were considering exporting a product to Europe, it is incredibly conceivable that you may run
into someone who is a business person who works out of Europe.
They may be on vacation here but overhear you talking and introduce
themselves. Consider every conversation a way to network. The person you are speaking to may know someone or know someone who
knows someone. This is the very nature of networking.

3.   *Your support group (see Chapter Four)* – If you have built up
a support group of businesses to work with, chances are they will also
know people to put you into contact with about becoming a business
partner or agent for you in the country or countries you are wanting to
build an exporting business with. For example, the shipper who you
partner with may have a local agent who has time to work for you as
well. Again, the key is to simply ask. If they do not know anyone you
are not out anything but the time it took to ask. Your support group is
also an excellent way to simply network. Again, they may not directly
know someone but can help spread the word that you are seeking a
partner or agent in a specific country.

4.   *Corporate Council of Africa*[1] – For those looking to export
goods and services to Africa, the Corporate Council of Africa is an
excellent starting place. Within the council are representatives from
many nations in Africa and they can provide potential business contacts for each country in Africa. They offer conferences in the United
States as well as other countries plus on-demand research to help facilitate partnerships. They also help assist members with finding trade
leads and business contacts.

5. **Country's Chamber of Commerce** – Almost every country has a chamber of commerce. One of the functions of this government body is to help foreign nationals and build the country's business and tourism industries. They will have contacts for business people in their country to help you develop business contacts within the country.

6. **Embassy contact** – As an ancillary to the chamber of commerce, many embassies have similar information as the country's chamber of commerce at their disposal. Writing, calling or, if feasible, visiting a prospective country's embassy is a great way to start developing a relationship with not only potential business representatives but with governmental representatives who can help make the entire process as easy and straightforward as possible when trying to create your business in their country. Alternately, contacting your country's embassy in the country that you are planning on doing business with can be a great source of business contacts for that country.[2]

Checking the Pool to Find the Perfect Match

Once you have created a pool of potential business partners you need to check them out to make sure they are legitimate and trustworthy people to do business with. For some, you may have gotten the recommendation to contact them from a trusted source. For others, such as the friend of a friend who contacts you through your networking, due diligence is required to make sure that person has the integrity you need to trust them with your business matters in that country.

There are many people out there, especially in the current world economy, who are looking to make a quick buck and in doing so will not represent you and your company properly. Even if you catch it quickly, it could damage your reputation in that country to such an extent that you can never fix the damage enough to make it profitable afterwards.

In your pursuit of trustworthy individuals to become partners with or to serve as your agents, publicly available resources are often available from either your country or the country you are intending to export to. They may make recommendations for further investigation and how to do so and may have information already available on people who work in the import business in that country.

That said, for most export business ventures, government agencies are going to be the best place to start. For U.S. residents, the U.S. embassy, consulate or diplomatic mission to a country is an excellent place to start[2]. They will be able to help research the candidates you have chosen and tell you if they are legitimate business people or scam artists.

For U.S. citizens, there is also the **U.S. Commercial Services**[3] that will help assist you in finding out whether the person or persons you are looking to utilize as agents are good choices. Finally, the **U.S. Export Import Bank**[4] is another excellent resource to utilize, especially when eyeing key markets that this bank focuses on. If you are looking to export an American made good or are wishing to import an American made good to your country, they will happily help in any way possible including possibly helping finance the venture.

Most first world nations offer similar services to their citizens. A quick web search for your country and search items such as commercial services, chamber of commerce or other similar search topics will yield results particular to your country.

CHAPTER SIX:

Establish an Office in a Foreign Country

When you are first starting out with your business, you will likely find that you can handle everything through your agent from afar with no need for an office. However, once business begins to pick up, you will find that establishing an office in the country you are doing business with can offer many benefits.

If you are on the fence, consider this: an office established in a foreign country doubles your exposure in that country. If you feel this could mean more conversions and better sales, you would be absolutely correct and why this may be optional at first but will become a necessity at some point if your business is successful.

Benefits of Establishing an Office in a Foreign Country

• Creates a Presence in That Country

Simply creating the office and having it staffed creates a tangible, in country experience for those who you are selling to. The office symbolizes commitment. By taking the time and money to establish an office, you are showing the clients that you are serious and only a drive away, rather than insulated by an ocean to any complaints or issues that could arise. The personal touch of having an in-country office is a powerful thing.

• Improves Sales Conversions

By offering the best, customer focused experience for your clients, you are going to build a relationship with them quicker than the competitor trying to do all of the legwork from afar via phone, fax and email. As was mentioned in chapter three, most countries prefer interaction based on a relationship, not just what is immediately best for the business. You may even have to charge slightly more to cover overhead; but you will convert more sales because you are able to serve the clients so much better. The security that an office gives a client makes it worth it to them many times to pay more for the same product. They know that your company will be available should there be a warranty issue come up or even for further business in the future.

• Office Costs Can Be Lower

Depending on where you are building your export business to, there is a good chance that you can save a great deal of money establishing an office in the country you are exporting to rather than the country you are in. Business costs such as rent, utilities and labor costs are lower in many nations compared to nations such as the United States or Europe.

There are tax incentives as well; from developing nations offering importers preferred tax status for building a business or simply avoiding high corporate and payroll taxes that many first-world nations will charge that less developed countries do not. For example, the United States has some of the highest corporate taxes in the world and currently there are considerations of raising them yet again. Check with your legal representation and accountant, but establishing an office in a foreign country can mean the business is located overseas and changes the amount of tax that will have to be paid in your native country for the profits from the business.

• Makes The Country's Government Happy

As mentioned previously, establishing an office in the country you are exporting to or intend to export to can net some tax incentives. Even if the government gives you tax incentives to build open a business in their country and build out an office, they know with building an office you are going to be investing in their country as well as creating jobs. From the rent you pay for your office space, to the contractors you hire to make the office usable to the employees you hire, you are helping build their economy and will be bringing in foreign dollars at first to do so.

Where to Establish a Business

The adage "Location, Location, Location" is incredibly important when establishing your foreign office. A local business person really has more flexibility than you will when finding an appropriate place for an office. Your requirements should include:

1.   Your office should be located in a city, preferably the capital city, where major international flights go in and out of the country.

There are a number of benefits from putting your office near a major airport. When you visit, your travel time and expenses are both cut down quite a bit. Being located near the international airport, especially, reduces the number of connecting flights which is where your luggage is most likely lost and adds expense. On top of this, the need for lengthy cab rides or the difficulty of securing a rental car is negated. If the office is close by, having your local agent pick you up becomes an option as well.

Choosing the capital city as your location makes good business sense as well. On top of being the most obvious place for international travel in the country, you will have easy access to the government agencies who you will likely have already communicated with. By being able to get in and have meetings with these agents in person, it can smooth over any miscommunications and gives the interaction a personal feel which can go a long way to smoothing over red tape.

2. Your office should be located near the National Embassy of your country of origin.

Many of the countries which you are considering for export are not going to be completely stable. Even countries with years of stability can explode into conflict because of a change of governmental leadership. Take Indonesia, for instance. Indonesia was stable for a number of years but about ten years ago this changed when the government changed hands. When this happened, many foreigners left and many did so very quickly. Having a National Embassy for your country of origin nearby gives you a safe haven should something go awry. This could be a large scale event such as a revolution or coup d'état or something as simple as you losing your passport.

For any country, regardless of the stability, the Embassy for your country of origin can be an excellent resource for your business as well. They will have contacts in the host country's government which they will share with you to help launch and maintain your business. As mentioned in previous chapters, they are an excellent resource for all things regarding the host country and visiting the Embassy in person only enhances the help they are willing to give you.

3. Your office should be located in a business district or other area associated with the business you are in.

This goes without saying but has to be addressed. With the focus of location related to airports as well as near your Nation's Embassy, it could be tempting to ignore being around businesses which deal in similar products or services when finding a location for your office.

Most cities have a business zone where most offices are setup and there may even be a specific area of the business zone for importers. This gives you an excellent chance to further network with other companies which have been doing business in the country and are established.

How to Establish a Foreign Office

The process of establishing your foreign office is pretty straightforward. If you intend to have an in country business partner or agent, they will likely be the one who helps establish the office as well as the one who works out of the office. It is best to make sure that the business is working and that the partner or agent is holding up their end of things before proceeding with them in the investment of an office or even warehouse space. Visiting the country and with the agent or partner in person during the first phase of the business is vital to making sure everything is running smoothly and helps with the decision making process of opening an office in the first place.

Should you decide to proceed, you will want to work with any legal help you have acquired as part of your team or support group. They will either know or be willing to do research into the rules and regulations which pertain to opening a business in the country you want to export to. The time and money spent looking into laws and regulations are vital to making sure your office opens on time and on budget.

Even things that seem mundane, such as getting a business license can be held up by red tape if diligent research is not done ahead of time to identify and work through the country's bureaucracy. Many countries also offer websites that give overview of the basics of establishing a business in their country.

For example, the **Russian American Chamber of Commerce** has information for many of the countries under its umbrella that will help get you started if those countries are ones you are interested in. Their website has an excellent write up for Armenia, for instance that includes information as detailed as incorporation fees and what types of corporations are allowed in the country[1]. **The Corporate Council of Africa** can help get this information to you as well[2].

Alternative to Establishing Your Own Foreign Office

Alternately, finding an established company with experience in the region which produces or imports some other type of goods could be an excellent way of not only reducing legwork on your part but gaining a number of benefits as well. For this type of deal you have to come up with a fee structure that is mutually beneficial for both you as well as the company you are partnering with and while you are sharing resources, you are also helping to promote their business as well. This can be the best way to penetrate the market in a country for which you have little previous experience with. The benefits of such an arrangement include:

1. Skips the Red Tape and Ground Work

Partnering with an established company gets rid of many hurdles that you would normally have to go through; not only with establishing a foreign office but in the overall scope of building your importing business in your chosen country. They have gone through the regulatory processes, secured the proper permits to operate and already have spent the time and money to make sure that all aspects of their business are following the laws and regulations of the country.

You are simply offering them a unique product or service that they do not handle and are offering to do all of the work regarding that product or service. It really is win-win. You get in without the legwork and they can rely on you talking them up during your business dealings in your chosen country.

2. Mentoring

On top of getting to use an existing company's ground work, most companies who are willing to help you are also going to be willing to invest a bit further by mentoring you. This could be informal help such as suggesting which language to try to learn to actually putting you into classes with their employees to learn the language. They will also already know the business culture as well as customs of the country and can help you on your way learning about these things.

3. Better and Quicker Relationship Formation

By working with an established company, you are essentially riding on their coattails. While not working directly for them, you will be working with them closely enough that their reputation in that country will carry you. When looking at companies to partner with, be sure to check their reputation because it can sink you if their reputation is tarnished. If you walk into a country and meet with business leaders or government representatives as a partner with a company with a good reputation, some of the relationship those people share with the company you are now affiliated with will be extended to you and what you are doing in the country.

There are even companies that specialize in the export/import business. If you are looking at expanding your current business globally, these companies can do all of the leg work for you by essentially becoming your contracted export department. From travel resources to client follow-up; not to mention working through a country's unique way of allowing business, this type of company could be a good match for some businesses and even some entrepreneurs.

CHAPTER SEVEN:

Take Advantage of Incentives Provided By Exporting To Foreign Country

One of the common themes you have probably noticed throughout this book is that there are trade gaps in almost every country. Countries with goods always want to open new avenues to help move those goods and there are many countries without the infrastructure to manufacture products that are clamoring for those products.

The ultimate purpose of this book is for you to connect a supply to an untapped demand. On both sides, there are an incredible number of incentives available to the business or entrepreneur that is willing to do the work of connecting an export to a market that wants that product or service. There is national and international support for getting your goods or services to a country and most countries are incredibly hospitable to businesses wanting to open up in their country as well.

Incentives and Help from Your Home Country and the International Community

Your home country, especially if it is one with a strong manufacturing sector, will have incentives to help encourage trade. Some of these may be to encourage export but some may even be to encourage imports from specific countries or regions that seem to need assistance or are underrepresented in the local market. For example, the *AGOA Act* allows imports from Africa to the United States to be imported duty free.

This encourages businesses to go to African nations and develop businesses overseas to import those products back into the United States without having to worry about paying duty taxes on the United States side. This increases the profit for the business and allows them to increase the capacity that they can afford.

Aside from some special import and duty fee waivers, the most common incentives available to a business or entrepreneur from their home country or world community are financial incentives. In previous chapters, it has been mentioned to find business partners that have money to invest. However, many countries have special governmental departments that have grants and loans at their disposal to help a company or entrepreneur begin an export business venture. Instead of a private corporation, it then becomes possible to essentially go into business with your home country's government instead.

In the United States, there is the ***Export/Import Bank***[1] which is an agency of the United States Federal government. Businesses and Entrepreneurs can utilize the ***Export/Import Bank*** in a couple of ways. They focus on helping clients in other countries purchase your goods. They do this by working directly with the client to allow them to buy your product directly from you in the United States.

An example of this usage would be a foreign airline using the ***Export/Import Bank's*** financing to purchase a plane from a company such as Boeing. While it is unlikely you are trying to move a multi-million dollar product, any business selling a product and is just beginning to get into exporting can help their client secure financing this way.

The second way that the ***Export/Import Bank*** works is they will give your company a line of credit that you can then extend to clients. If you have inventory in your destination country, this allows your company the flexibility of offering financing through the ***Export/Import Bank*** to customers that need credit to purchase your product. For Example, a car company with a dealership in a foreign country would likely be utilizing the ***Export/Import Bank*** as their lending service to finance vehicles in that country.

Most first world nations have similar government run banking programs to help businesses make their products available internationally. Doing a search through a web search engine for your home country will let you know if this resource is available in your home country though most first-world nations have them now.

The next resource available to exporters from the United States is **OPIC,** or the **Overseas Private Investment Corporation**[2]. For exporters that want to work in developing countries or those that are transitioning from nonmarket to market economies, **OPIC** can be an excellent resource. **OPIC** offers not only loans but also grants and even some insurance forms. They do have some pretty strict requirements to be eligible. At the moment, the requirements are:

• *There must be a foreign partner*

• *There must be a United States Citizen that is a partner*

• *OPIC will fund 60% of the project, the remainder of the 40% of the funding must be provided by the partners. 25% of that funding must be from the United States partner.*

• *The United States partner must have 20% ownership or more in the project.*

• *The private sector of banks must have been contacted and are unwilling to take on the risk.*

There are projects that **OPIC** cannot help corporations take on but are related to large-scale environmental impact issues and military production and sales. **OPIC** is an excellent resource for any venture that meets the criteria though; even if for the political upheaval insurance that they offer.

The World Bank[3] is the final place for incentives that are not in the destination country. The **World Bank and the International Finance Corporation**[4] offer interest free and low interest loans to businesses and entrepreneurs to help them open businesses in developing country. If your business will help improve the quality of life in the target developing country; or you intend on exporting from that country to a developed country, the **IFC** can help with different incentives. From low interest loans to open your business to helping extend credit to clients, similar to the Export/Import Banks, they have many options available to help your business venture.

"When doing business, do business with people who have money."
— Andrew Morrison

Destination Country Incentives

Most countries work hard to get foreign businesses to investors to come into their country. For them, it becomes an excellent way to bring in capital and help their economy. Because of this, they are willing to offer incentives to help encourage business. There are a number of different incentives that countries will offer up to encourage development in their country from foreign business interests:

Aside from the tax benefits that are covered in detail in chapter eight, there are other ways that your target country will be willing to help you out. Of these, the two most significant are land benefits as well as financial transaction incentives. Research will be required to find these programs. For most countries, the government is essentially a one-stop-shop for information about what services and incentives they provide and what requirements you will have to meet for your business to be eligible. If you have done all of your other homework, much of this should be in place before your first meeting with the government contact you find.

Land benefits can be severely discounted purchase or lease terms for government land for development of warehouse or office space. If your business plan or model involves storing inventory, building up from scratch could become much more affordable than you would think if the land is practically given to you compared to renting existing space.

Financial transaction incentives include tax breaks (more in chapter eight) as well as other breaks. One big one that some countries offer is more favorable currency conversion rates for businesses compared to tourists. They will exchange the money without any fees or conversion tariffs to help businesses keep their money working. Further transaction incentives would be waiving fees and tariffs on out of country money transfers that most countries charge banks.

CHAPTER EIGHT:

Take Advantage of Tax Incentives for Exporting

Both in your country as well as the country you are working with, there are tax incentives that you will be able to take advantage of. For both sides of the supply and demand table, they are motivated to try to find ways to make the connection between them lucrative for the person willing to take on such a business venture. For you or your business that is targeting this connection, these tax incentives come in a number of forms:

1. Getting Your Goods from Your Home Country to Its Destination Tax Free

Most developed nations, due to their trade deficits, are willing to sacrifice taxes on exports to help make the exporting process as trouble free and cost-free as possible. The United States, for instance, has absolutely no taxes levied on exports from the United States. Many other countries share this philosophy or at least share it to a certain extent. The use of export taxes is a way to encourage some industries by offering little or no taxes on those items, while curtailing the export of other items. Sometimes, these incentives are setup by the host nation while others are setup by trade treaties that have been signed between the two nations.

2. Getting Your Goods into the Destination Country Tax Free

There a couple ways that a business can avoid paying taxes on their goods, also know as duties, that they are importing into a country. First of all, many import taxes are waived because of trade treaties or legislation passed in the country. For instance, the United States has treaties with Canada and Mexico through the **NAFTA**[1] (**North Atlantic Free Trade Agreement**) treaty and with most of Africa through the **AGOA**[2] (**African Growth and Opportunity Act**). For the countries covered under these pieces of legislation, there are no duties to be paid for importing from those countries to the United States.

The second way to get your goods into the destination country tax free is to establish your foreign office in a duty free zone. These zones are designed to encourage growth of foreign businesses and help build the economy and infrastructure by helping get more imports into the country. This should be considered a mandatory part of your research into finding a location for your foreign office or warehouse.

A country may build a new port facility and will, to encourage development around the port, offer duty free zones for a set amount of time or indefinitely for the area around the port. Timing is everything and getting in on the ground floor of such a deal will pay off, even if your imports fail to impress the country's customers. Your fallback will be the real estate that you have that is in that duty-free zone.

The third way to keep from being taxed on your imports into the destination country is to avoid goods that are taxed. Some countries will allow items into the country but charge heavy duty's on them to discourage importation of those items. India, for instance, has incredibly high tariffs on imports of used vehicles from other markets. This is done to protect the growing car industry in India from a flood of cheap imported cars that could easily flood the market and prevent the growth of the home-grown industry.

While protectionist in nature, for the business person looking for something to import into India, they will see the duty on car imports and decide very quickly that importing cars into India makes no business sense whatsoever. During your research into the country and their needs, also consider the tax implications of the goods you are wishing to export to the country.

3.   Other Tax Incentives

On top of the tax incentives that a country gives on the product that you are importing and exporting, many countries will offer other types of tax incentives to new businesses that open up in their country. These incentives include reduced payroll, business, corporate or income tax rates or, at the least, a greater number of tax write-offs during the first few years of being in business in that country.

Finding Tax Incentives

In a word, finding these tax incentives requires research. Much of the research into finding tax incentives will be part of research that you are doing into other avenues of the countries and products that you are considering. However, because the governments are the ones that create and collect the taxes, the best source for finding tax incentives is the government.

Your nation's embassy for the country is an excellent place to start. They will have governmental contacts for the host country's government; not to mention research of their own that they have done for other businesses. Part of an embassy's job is to help facilitate business growth in the host nation.

As you are building your support group of companies, as outlined in chapter four, finding legal and accounting advice for the country you want to export to can become a valuable asset for this process as well. Because they work in the country and know the laws and regulations, they will be aware of the newest tax laws, how to maximize your profit and find every tax incentive you can use. Your time spent researching and finding legal and accounting professionals in the destination country will culminate when they begin working to find tax incentives for your business.

CHAPTER NINE:

Take Advantage of Trade Financing

Trade financing allows you to use other people's money in order to conduct business when exporting to another country. Without trade financing you may find that your ability to export is greatly curtailed. This is especially true for start up companies with little to no capital or small to medium sized businesses wishing to go global.

You can use trade financing to reduce transaction costs and facilitate an expedited shipping process. Exporters will often need working capital in order to manufacture the goods and get them to shipment prior to receiving payment from the buyer. Trade financing allows the exporter to extend credit or await payment for a reasonable time instead of demanding pre payment for the sale. This is a more favorable arrangement for most consumers. If there is no trade financing available it can sorely limit the amount of exporting that occurs and can slow or severely damage the economy of a country.

Trade Financing Instruments

Documentary credit is the most common form of the commercial letter of credit. The way it works is the issuing bank makes a payment and this is paid out only upon the presentation of particular documents. The bank is loaning money to the importer and is responsible for paying the exporter.

Counter trade is another financing instrument where the importer and exporter barter without any exchange of money. For example, the exporter has a particular good the importer needs. The importer has a separate good the exporter needs. They trade an equitable amount of goods without issuing any money.

How the Government Can Help

Many countries offer trade financing subsidized by the government in order to encourage trade and boost the economy. Government subsidized trade financing can be accomplished individually or in conjunction with partner private banks.

The Export-Import Bank (EXIM Bank) is an especially good source of government funding to importers and exporters. They provide a variety of services to help the exporter including direct loans and export credit guarantees.[1]

CHAPTER TEN:

Travel to Enhance your Business

Setting up and maintaining a global business will require you to travel at times. It may even require you to set up an office in a foreign country and even to move there to live part time or full time. There are many advantages to travelling in order to enhance your business but you have to be smart about it. You do not want all your profits getting eaten up by travel expenses so you need to make the most of your time and maximize the opportunity for travel.

Benefits of Foreign Travel

There are many benefits to foreign travel. When you take the time to meet with your partners as well as your clients you have an invaluable opportunity to solidify relationships and increase your business through networking. Trust is established. Operations can be overseen in person. It is not a matter of travelling if you have the chance. You should instead see foreign travel as a necessary expenditure to increase your business. Some advantages include:

> • *When you travel to foreign countries it allows you to interact with your foreign clients helping you to establish and maintain solid relationships.*

> • *It allows you to put a face to a name when it comes to your business associates.*

> • *You can get a feel for foreign partners to ensure they are authentic and have your best interests at heart.*

> • *You can interact with employees to further instill a sense of loyalty to the business.*

• *You can personally deal with any issues that arise ensuring the problems are addressed in a timely manner.*

• *You can evaluate the daily operations of the business and get a fuller idea of how improvements can be made.*

• *It allows you to increase your customer base and your market by allowing you to personally network with clients.*

• *A client or business partner is more liable to trust you when they get one on one interaction in person.*

Maximize your Travel Time

When you travel you will spend a lot of time in airports, transferring planes and sitting on a plane while waiting to arrive at your destination. This may seem like a lot of time that is wasted but it can be a great opportunity to conduct business. The time away from the office gives you solitude to consider your business and make plans. But it also allows you an opportunity to network and make new and potentially valuable new relationships. Use the travel time to your benefit. Maximize the opportunities it affords you:

• *You will likely meet other business people in your travels. Use this opportunity to network.*

• *Introduce yourself to others and strike up conversations. You never know where you might find a valuable employee, business partner, vendor or even a customer.*

• *Conduct work while travelling. Take your laptop with you and catch up on any work that you have been putting off because of pressing matters in the office requiring your attention.*

• *Reply to any outstanding emails or written correspondence. This is the perfect "quiet time" opportunity to do so.*

• *Catch up on industry reading. This is a great time to educate yourself on emerging trends or advancing technology that could enhance your business.*

• *Review your business plan and note how you may want to make changes for future growth. Start making notes now so you are prepared for later.*

• *Plan the week, month or year ahead. Make lists of important tasks or goals you want to accomplish. If you have made previous goal lists review them to see where you stand and what is outstanding to do.*

• *Use the time travelling to market yourself. You can write industry related articles or blogs to publish on social networking sites or industry periodicals that will point back to your business website and establish you as an expert in the field. This will expand your global presence.*

• *Brush up on the country's culture. Be aware of any social etiquette that will be important when meeting with people residing in the country. You do not want to make any faux pas and this is the ideal time to ensure you know everything you need to avoid such.*

• *Use the time to study the language of the country. Even if you can only manage a few simple phrases or greetings, the effort you put forth will be appreciated. With each trip you can expand this knowledge until you are a fluent speaker of the language.*

• *Pack a pen and pad of paper. If you are in an area where you can not use your electronic devices a pen and paper will still work marvelously.*

• *Make sure you have a business mindset for your trip. This is not vacation time so do not set aside time for sight seeing or tourism. Remember you are working just as if you were in your office at home.*

• *Fill your day with meetings and activities pertaining to work. Schedule these ahead of time and ensure you have a solid day's worth of meetings and networking so you can increase business.*

Tips to Save Money Travelling on Business

With the economy, inflation and the increasing cost of fuel travel is not cheap. In fact it can be very expensive. Even though there are some extremely lucrative opportunities that arise from business travel and travelling can be highly advantageous, you do not want all your profits depleted by travel expenses. So, just as you should maximize your time during travel so you are not wasting it so too should you maximize your money. The key to international travel is to save money and get things done. Travel smart so you can minimize expense:[1]

• *Don't fly first class. There is no need to be flashy and the added expense can be exorbitant.*

• *Check with the refund policies of multiple airlines. It is almost always cheaper to purchase a non refundable ticket so do that whenever possible but some airlines will allow you to change or cancel your flight with little to no penalty if the amount is applied to a future ticket.*

• *If you can maximize your time wisely, you may not mind the added time spent for connecting flights. While direct flights are more convenient and will get you there faster, making a stop or two will save you a considerable amount of money.*

• *Shop around for your flights and compare round trip against two single one way flights. Sometimes there can be a difference.*

• *Book your flight in advance.*

• *Try to have as much flexibility in your travel schedule as possible. You can use name your own price travel sites and compare travel expenses during various departure days when you have some flexibility.*

• *Negotiate corporate rates with hotel chains.*

• *Stay at hotels that are not in the center of the city. It is often cheaper to stay a bit off the beaten path and rent a car than to get a hotel in the hub of the city.*

• *Corporate housing can often offer discounts that are far better than a full service hotel.*

• *Use public transportation when possible.*

• *Consider alternate modes of travel especially when travelling from one country to another on an extended trip. Trains are often a lot cheaper than air.*

CHAPTER ELEVEN:

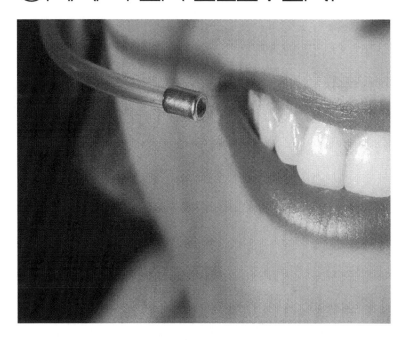

The Importance of Customer Service

Most business people are familiar with the statistic of, "it costs five times as much to bring in a new customer, than to keep an existing one."[1] With such a philosophy it is no wonder so many successful businesses concentrate on providing exceptional customer service to their clients.

With global businesses this is no different. There are several aspects of customer service that need to be addressed in order to ensure your customers remain with you and have a sense of loyalty.

Always keep in mind that customers have a tendency to relay their experiences with companies. They are especially likely to tell others when there is an exceptionally positive experience or an exceptionally negative one. You want to strive for your customers to tell others how great you are to help garner referrals. You do not want your customers telling others not to do business with you because of a poor customer service experience. So, to avoid this, take action and make sure your customer service policies are in place.

> *"There is only one boss. The customer. And he can fire
> everybody in the company from the chairman on down,
> simply by spending his money somewhere else."*
> — *SAM WALTON*[2]

First is not Always Best

Just because you are the first at something does not mean you are automatically the best. In fact, if you are first, you may have a tougher time of it than competitors coming in to take a portion of your market share. The reason for this is that they have an advantage of seeing any errors you have made along the way and implementing policies and procedures to avoid these mistakes from the onset. So, just because you are the first supplier in a country of a particular product, do not take this for granted and put your customer satisfaction priorities on the back burner.

You will get competition. It may not be today or tomorrow but it will happen. Eventually someone will come along who will want a slice of the pie. In order to get a piece of your existing market share, though, they will have to do something better. Perhaps they are more efficient and provide quality products at a lesser cost. However, even if you are slightly more expensive, if you have achieved customer loyalty you will likely not see a vast decrease in clientele. If you start building that customer loyalty now, your customer will not move to your competition.

If, however, you have slacked on implementing customer service policies you are in for difficult times. You may currently have 100% of the market share in your industry in that country. But it is due to you being the only supplier, not because you are the best. Once competition comes in that will provide a comparable product with quality customer service, you will see that share dwindle considerably. So, if you are first, implement strong customer service policies now. Instill a sense of loyalty in your customers so when (not if) competition comes, you will not lose your customer base.

> *You'll never have a product or price advantage again.*
> *They can be easily duplicated, but a strong customer service*
> *culture can't be copied.*
> *— JERRY FRITZ*[3]

Employees are the Back Bone of Your Company

One of the first steps you need to implement when constructing your customer policies is a favorable environment for your employees. They are the backbone of your company and they will be the ones dealing with your customers on a daily basis. If they are treated well then they will be more likely to have a positive impact on your customer service. However, if they do not have any sense of loyalty to your company then they won't care if your customers are treated well. To do this, make sure you treat your employees well, give them the necessary tools to do their job effectively, listen to feedback from those who work with your customers every day and monitor your staff for their performance.

Employee Satisfaction

If your employees like their job then this is a bonus and they will work harder for you. However, let's face it, nobody works for free and nobody wants to be under valued. So, first and foremost, make sure you pay your employees fairly.4 Consider the market and the economy of the country you are working in. Pay your employees a fair wage and offer benefits as needed. Salary and benefits are of prime importance for recruiting and retaining quality employees but it does not stop there. You also need to provide a positive work environment for your employees so they will be happy with their job overall.

Even though employment laws will vary from country to country do not take advantage of labor laws that allow you to treat your employees unfairly. Make sure they work a fair amount of hours per day and week so they are not over burdened. Make sure your senior personnel and management team treat the employees fairly. Avoid conflicts and make the work environment as pleasant as possible. If you have the right balance of wage and environment, your quality personnel will strive to make your company as great as it can be.

Without great employees you can never have great customer service.
— RICHARD F. GERSON[2]

Training

If your employees have a sense of loyalty this is half the battle. However, even if your employees have the desire to treat your customers well it will not do a bit of good unless they are provided with the tools necessary to implement your customer service policies. Training is essential in order to provide your employees with your philosophies on how to treat customers as well as practical application of those policies. First, make sure your employees are well versed on the products or services you sell so they can take care of your customers' needs. You need to make sure you have a sound, written customer service policy that your employees are familiar with and that you make sure your employees are trained on how to implement those policies for varying scenarios.

Also, empower your employees according to their level to make autonomous decisions. If you have a hierarchy of employees from the first line to senior management, each party can resolve issues with customers and make decisions according to their position. If need be, they can pass on a customer to someone in a superior position if the need arises. Make sure your employees are familiar with how to handle each customer and how to deal with internal policies as well.

Take Suggestions

As a president, owner or CEO of a company you are likely not the person dealing with the daily interaction of your customers. You rely instead on your first line of employees. This may also mean that you are somewhat disconnected from your customers. But that first line of employees is not and often your best ideas on how to better improve your customer service will come from them. Encourage an environment where suggestions are welcome. Listen to your employees when they make a suggestion and implement the ones that are sound. You may find that some of your best changes are due to feedback you receive from those working with your customers on a daily basis.

Monitor, Evaluate and Take Action

You need to always know where your employees stand and how well they are doing. This will help during evaluation times and to determine the amount of any merit raises or bonuses you feel are warranted. It will also tell you which employees are not living up to their potential and which are a detriment to your business. So, the first thing you need to do is monitor the employees' performance. Make sure you are aware of how each employee interacts with customers, how well they follow policy and whether or not they go above and beyond the scope of their duties.

Once you know how each employee interacts and deals with customers, you can evaluate their performance. There will typically be a wide spectrum of results. Once you have this evaluation complete you need to take action and let your employees know how they are doing. You will have the majority of your employees who do a good job according to the letter of their job duties. Let them know they are doing well and give them suggestions on how to improve further. You may want to reward these employees with a somewhat standard merit pay increase when it is time for this.

Some employees will show excellence when dealing with customers. You may have customers who send in positive reviews of a particular employee or you may see someone who has saved a customer on multiple occasions due simply to their finesse in dealing with them. These employees should be in some way rewarded. You can do this verbally, by a special recognition, tangible reward, bonus, above average merit pay increase or promotion. Letting them know gives them the confidence to continue and lets other employees see a good example and how that is rewarded.

You will also likely have a few employees from time to time who offer sub standard performance when dealing with customer support. It is then your job to determine if the employee is salvageable or needs to be let go. You have already invested in the employee so it usually benefits to try to improve their work. Perhaps more training is needed or more supervision. Attempt this tactic first and if it does not work, perhaps termination is in order.

However, there will be occasions where the error is so grievous that the employee needs to be terminated immediately. If so, take action and do so. It is better to lose an employee than to lose a customer or multiple customers because of their actions. After evaluating the performance of your employees take action with praise rewards, additional guidance or in some cases, termination. If your work force is superior, your customers will notice.

Customer Communication

One of the first policies to implement when dealing with customer service is your philosophy on communication with your customer. Typically you will have contact in person as well as via telephone and email. Each person responsible for this aspect should be aware of how to deal with your customers appropriately.

Be Friendly

It is often said that customer service with a smile makes all the difference. It may sound silly but it is true. If you deal with your customers while smiling, whether in person or not, this will be conveyed to the customer. The customer will have a pleasant experience and come away feeling satisfied. Be courteous and professional but also make it personal. The customer wants to feel special and that you are catering to them. This is easy to do with a pleasant attitude even in the face of an irate customer. The philosophy is simple: be friendly. The practical side of always being friendly may not be as easy but with some practice it will become second nature.

In-Person Etiquette

When your customer is face to face with you, this provides the best opportunity to make a great impression and to be personable. However, it may also pose the most challenges if the customer is difficult to deal with or has a complaint. It is much easier to mask frustration and annoyance over the phone or via an email than it is in person. Always be helpful and pleasant when dealing with customers. Greet the customer warmly and pay attention to their needs. If you have limited staff, make sure to greet those who are waiting and get to them promptly when you are done dealing with the previous customer.

Telephone Etiquette

It is often easy to become distracted when on the phone especially if you are located in a busy call center. However, it is very important to pay attention to the caller and focus on the issue at hand. Avoid distractions and ensure your work area is conducive to such. Do not have entertainment sites on your computer. Do not read or look at magazines during work hours when you are answering the phone.

Make sure your tone of voice is professional and pleasant. Do not eat, drink or chew gum while on the phone. The person at the other end of the line will get an immediate impression of you and subsequently your company by your tone of voice alone. If you are courteous, articulate and professional you will sound like you know what you are talking about and instill a sense of confidence in the customer. Practice taking calls and dealing with situations to perfect your telephone voice and how to act while on the phone.[5]

Online Etiquette

In today's technological age more people are using the Internet to communicate with their customers. Forums, chat programs and email are especially prevalent forms of online communication these days. Unfortunately, a lot of these same systems are used for personal communication and some bad habits have been formed because of it. Consider online media in the same light as any other. You need to be professional and courteous.

In order to do this the number one rule is to avoid net speak6. Net speak is the way some people communicate on the Internet as an alternate to proper grammar. Often acronyms, symbols, numbers, misspellings and abbreviations are used. There is often little to no punctuation or capitalization used. Actions are expressed through words as if the person receiving the words can see the action. There is also an informality that is prevalent. These short cuts are fine for entertainment and personal communication but not acceptable for professional use.

For example:

> Hi, how r u?
>
> Wots up?
>
> Will u b home @ 4 pm 2 call u back?
>
> Lemme check on that
>
> Sorry 2 hear that
>
> LOL (laughing out loud), OMG (oh my god), BRB (be right back)

The above examples should never be used in professional communication. Even if your customers chat or email you with such terms, you should always reply in a professional manner. It will make you look more intelligent and will leave a good impression.

> *If you make customers unhappy in the physical world, they might each tell 6 friends. If you make customers unhappy on the Internet, they can each tell 6,000 friends.*
> *— JEFF BEZOS[2]*

What Not to Do

When you are practicing customer service skills, there are some things you want to avoid. In such cases it may be tempting to say them or do them but if you use an alternate choice the reaction from customers will be much more favorable. Always consider that you want the customer to leave the conversation regardless of the mode of communication with a positive outlook of you and the company.

Customer Service Best Practices Chart

DO NOT...	INSTEAD...
Say "I don't know"	Say "Let me find out for you". Try to get an answer from someone who knows so you have the answer for future customers who may ask that question. Take notes and create a cheat sheet.
Transfer a customer to someone else without verifying the transfer	Apologize for having to transfer them, stay on the line until connected and make introductions as necessary.
Make a customer wait too long	Request a call back number so you can research and then call back as soon as possible.
Say "I can't do that".	Say, "This is what I can do". This conveys a more positive attitude and indicates that you are doing something to resolve the issue.
Say "Just a second" or "I'll be right back" if you are unsure how long you will be.	Give an accurate time frame of when you will return to them with an answer. If you are taking longer than expected get back with them, apologize for taking so long and ask if they mind waiting a bit longer.
Lie	Be honest in your dealings with people even if you have bad news to convey. People will appreciate honesty even if it is not what they want to hear.
Say "No".	The word "no" is negative. Instead, spin it to use positive words using alternative solutions.

Establish a Complaint Resolution Process

Inevitably you will have a customer who is not satisfied with the level of service they received or the quality of the product you sold them. Sometimes this is your fault and sometimes not but regardless laying blame is not the answer. Instead, you need to have a process for dealing with complaints so the issues are dealt with in an expedient manner and resolved to the satisfaction of the customer.

Believe it or not sometimes a complaint will lead to even more business. Most customers realize that behind the business name are people and people sometimes make mistakes. If a problem is resolved quickly and to a customer's satisfaction this will often make them even more confident that they made the correct choice in using your company over another's. Do not look at complaints as a negative, instead look at it as a means to improve your company and add value to it.

> *Customers don't expect you to be perfect.*
> *They do expect you to fix things when they go wrong.*
> *—DONALD PORTER*[3]

Listen to your Customer

The first thing you need to establish is a method of communicating a customer's complaint to the appropriate party. This is either done via telephone, the Internet or in person. Ideally, you will have all methods to make it as easy as possible for your customers to communicate with you. After you have established the method for communicating complaints you then need to make responses a priority. Make sure all responses are timely and thorough.

When you receive a complaint it is essential to listen to your customer. Allow them to vent if they need to and empathize with their problem even if it is something that is not necessarily your fault. Do not interrupt the customer while they are talking because this will lead to even more frustration. Plus, you want to ensure you get the entire picture so you can fully deal with it. Take notes and then repeat the issue to your customer. Apologize for the problem they are having and then work on resolving the issue.[1]

For example, if your customer has a problem because the product you sent them is not performing as expected, apologize for the issue and repeat, in your own words what the problem is. Once this is done, let them know you will work on resolving it for them. A response may sound like, "Mr. Jones, you are having a problem because the part that was not sent is not working properly, correct?" After the acknowledgement or further clarification, "I am sorry you are having this problem, let me see what can be done about that."

Resolve the Issue

There are many ways a problem can be resolved and you need to have clear policies of what to do in each situation. Do your best to resolve the issue to the customer's satisfaction and go the extra mile if need be to make the customer happy. Do not lay blame on the customer or make excuses, simply do your best to clarify or take care of the problem. Above all be honest. Make sure the customer is well aware of how you will resolve the issue and how long it will take to accomplish. Even if the customer is angry, they will be even more so if you lie to them. This will exacerbate a situation and turn a potentially favorable outcome into a negative one.

When you have completed communicating to your customer how you intend to resolve the issue, make sure the resolution is acceptable to them. Get their approval and notate it on their account notes in case someone else has to look up the customer and speak with them. Then, make sure to follow through with your promises and resolve the issue. If the resolution is not immediate, follow up with the customer as soon as it is complete to ensure they are aware the resolution is complete and to get their approval once again. Even though you are resolving a problem, this is also a great opportunity to reinforce the relationship and can go a long way in instilling a sense of confidence and customer loyalty.[1]

> *One customer, well taken care of, could be more valuable than $10,000 worth of advertising.*
> *— JIM ROHN*[2]

Dealing with Irate Customers

Many times, customers who have a complaint will explain it calmly and expect a reasonable resolution. However, there will be times when you get a customer complaint where they are extremely irate and even yelling at you. Of primary importance is that you keep your cool and do not overreact to the situation. Your job is to diffuse the situation and leave the customer happy in the end. This will take some tact and finesse but it is not an impossible feat.

First, allow the customer to vent and do not interrupt. If you interrupt you will make the customer angrier and it will escalate an already bad situation. Instead, simply let the customer vent about the problem. Empathize with the customer and apologize then assure them you will do everything you can to help them and resolve the issue. Keep calm and align yourself with them. Do not allow yourself to be baited if a customer becomes abusive. If necessary, transfer them to a supervisor who is better versed in handling these escalated calls. If you do need to transfer the call, explain to the customer that you want to be sure this is expedited and will transfer the customer to a member of management who can better assist them.

Know your Customer

In order to improve customer service you need to know who your customers are and what their needs are. If you do not know your customers you can not effectively serve them and give them quality service. To do this you should first listen to your employees who deal with your customers on a daily basis. But, you also need to listen to your customers directly and one way to do this is to allow feedback, both positive and negative. You should also have a database of your customers where you can easily gather demographic information and buying trends. This information will help you get to know your customers, their habits and their needs.

Gather Feedback

There are many ways you can gather feedback. One way is to use polls. Make sure the polls are optional and unobtrusive. Gather a list of questions and ask for feedback on how your customers think your service can be improved. You should also have an easy to find feedback form on your website so that customers can leave positive feedback or suggestions when they feel the need to do so. This will tell you where you are going right and where you can improve. Also, have a centralized location for employees at a call center or retail location to enter suggestions they have received verbally by customers.

Incentives

You can use customer data to provide incentives to customers. You can reward valuable customers who have been utilizing your services for some time or who have purchased a certain amount of product. This shows the customer you appreciate their business. You can also see which customers have not dealt with your company in awhile and contact them to see if you can be of service. You can even send customers messages for birthdays or other important events. This lends a personal touch and will enhance the relationship with your customers.

Some examples of incentives to customers include:

- *Personalized notes thanking them for their business*
- *Coupons*
- *Holiday greetings*
- *Gifts and trinkets such as T-shirts, coffee mugs or mouse pads with your logo on them.*

Satisfaction Guaranteed

Customer service is very important and it should be continually reevaluated. Start off with policies and procedures that will work for your business model but do not be so rigid as to be against change. Instead, continually strive to improve so that you can stay on top of the latest trends and ensure your customers are always satisfied. Keep in mind that the business climate is continually changing. Sometimes your customer service policies will need to change with it. Set up reviews of your policies and listen to feedback. With the data you have you can see what is working and what needs to be improved. If you make customer service a priority, you will have happy, loyal customers who will not only continue to do business with you but will also refer you to others.

> *Unless you have 100% customer satisfaction…you must improve.*
> **HORST SCHULZ**[2]

CHAPTER TWELVE:

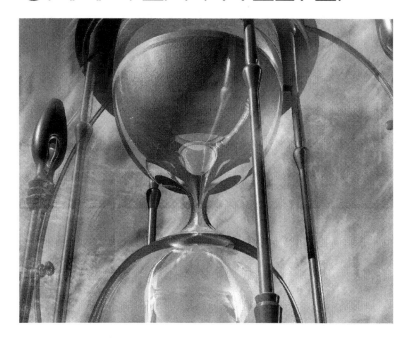

Deliver on Time, Every Time

In the United States most people have a sense of urgency and immediacy. Customers want instant gratification therefore most U.S. based businesses do their best to offer that. However, when dealing with foreign countries the sense of urgency may not be present. Some cultures simply do not have this concept. But, just because the culture does not adhere to stringent time schedules does not mean your company does not have to. In the world of international business being on time is a must. Exceed the expectations of your customers and work efficiently to maximize your time management. Make your company the one that sets itself apart by going against the norm in a positive way.

> *Here is a simple but powerful rule - always give people*
> *more than what they expect to get.*
> *— NELSON BOSWELL[1]*

The Importance of Delivering on Time

If you deliver on time, every time and especially if you exceed your delivery expectations you will enhance your business. You will establish a sense of trust that you are a reliable service to count on and that you can be trusted with important needs. Your reputation will grow considerably which can only benefit you. Because you benefit others, your own business will benefit. Businesses that use your services will refer you to others when the need arises. A referral is the best way to increase your business and attain additional quality customers.[2]

Deliver What on Time?

Deliver **everything** on time. If you have a request for a quote or pro-posal, make sure you have a rapid turn around time. Have you missed a call and need to return a customer query? Return it as soon as possi-ble. Do you have emails in your inbox? Reply to them immediately. Do you have shipments waiting? Get them out to your customers so they arrive on or before their expected delivery date. Make sure your customers have an idea of when you will deliver your promised good be it the actual product you sold, a quote or reply. You can post this on your website or have it as part of your internal policies and proce-dures.

Once you have posted, internally, externally or both, your delivery policies make sure you meet them at the very least. However, the true goal is to exceed them. If you have a policy where you turn around a quote in twenty four hours, strive to get it out the same day. If you reply to emails and telephone calls within six hours, make it one. If delivery will take a week, make it a few days. The more you exceed the expectations of your customers, the more confidence they will have in your company and the more likely they will be to use you again and refer you to others who may need your services.

Follow Up

When you make a delivery make sure you also follow up with your customers. This allows you a great opportunity to further establish your reputation and enhance the relationship between you and your customer. Verify that the customer received what they needed first. A conversation may go something like, "Mr. Jones, I see that you request-ed a quote for services. We sent the quote yesterday and I am calling to verify you received it, to see if you have any questions or if there is anything else I can help you with." Such a call will instill a sense of confidence in your company and give the customer an opportunity to ask any questions.

This is a great time to finalize a deal or practice good customer service policies. You have the opportunity to close a sale immediately, get additional business or simply leave a positive impression with the customer. If there is a problem you can address it and resolve it immediately before the customer has to initiate communication in the form of a complaint. Being proactive about your deliveries in the form of following up will cost you less in the long run and will potentially increase your sales as well as enhance your reputation.3

The Culture of the Company does not Value Timeliness

There are several countries where time is not a factor in their culture. They take their time; they do not keep set schedules and have low expectations for delivery schedules. If this is the case then you have a perfect opportunity to exceed the expectations of the businesses and consumers within that country. However, just because the country's culture is like this does not mean that every business or consumer in that country has the same philosophy. Do not get complacent with delivery schedules because of this.

Just as you are expanding into other countries so too will other businesses. U.S. based businesses as well as other countries with similar structures working in this country already have high expectations on delivery schedules and simply running out of another country does not change this. They are used to getting their emails replied to, phone calls responded to and their products delivered on time. Do not decrease the quality of your service just because the culture condones it. Instead, stick with your promises.

U.S. Based Businesses Selling to Foreign Countries

Another aspect of delivering on time that you need to take into consideration is the time differences between countries. This is especially true if you are a U.S. based business with no local office in the country you are dealing with. Keep in mind that while you may be shipping out the same day, it is already close of business in the country you are dealing with. So, you need to work efficiently for the country you are working with. If you promise a call by 9:00 am, you may be making that call in the middle of the night where you are located.

Keep time and date reminders so that you are well aware of what time it is in the different countries you deal with. If you need to ship or communicate with customers in that region, arrange your work schedule to accommodate those time differences. Not only will time be a factor between countries but local holidays and celebrations as well. Just as Thanksgiving Day in the United States is strictly celebrated in the U.S. other countries have honored days for that country alone. Make sure you are well aware of those.

During such times you may not be able to get work completed because businesses are closed. Or, it may be a cultural faux pas to attempt to conduct business during these times. You can avoid any delays or offenses by researching the country and keeping your calendar updated with any local holidays that may prevent your business from dealing efficiently and effectively with entities within the country.

Work Efficiency to Promote Timely Delivery

It is highly important to exceed expectations of delivery times. However, doing so may incur some additional overhead costs. But, this can be diminished by working more efficiently. Do not work more, work better. You should look at the efficiency in your company, cut out any unnecessary steps, streamline your processes and manage your time properly. If you do this, you can deliver on time, every time without incurring additional expense.

Time Management

In today's busy work climates many lament that there are not enough hours in the day. But do you really need more hours? You probably do not but instead need to manage your daily activities more efficiently to get the most out of the time you do have. Planning and organization are key elements to time management. Within that framework you need to know how to prioritize so that you can maximize the use of your time. You will also find that your productivity increases when you manage time properly. You will meet goals and exceed your delivery expectations.[4]

Organization

Before you can do anything you need to be organized. If you have a few tasks that are similar in function, effort and work, it is better to schedule them for completion together. This is because you will be in the same concentration wavelength and will be able to complete all the tasks together rather than having to complete them one at a time.

If you attempt to complete each task individually at different times of the day, you find that you have to waste time getting into the mindset each time you set about completing each task. Moreover, when you concentrate on similar tasks together, you are least likely to get interrupted by any outside intrusion.

However, you can not account for everything when scheduling your work load. Therefore, it is important to add some flexibility in your schedule for the unexpected. If you overbook you run the risk of not getting everything done or getting it done poorly.

Prioritization

You also need to learn to prioritize your work. Aim for taking care of the crucial work first and then the work that is not so much a priority. If you do this, you can make sure everything gets done on time without worrying about missing any important deadlines. While there are some who take care of the easy, less important work because it gets a lot accomplished in a short period of time, you may find that near the end of the day you are pressed for time, rushing and not utilizing the time to your best benefit.

Learn how to evaluate how important a task is based on how long it will take and the consequences involved in not getting it done on time. Leave room for fitting in emergency scenarios but you should have a general idea of the daily tasks you need to accomplish and when they should be done as well as the projects that may change from day to day.

Be Aware of Constraints

Make sure when prioritizing and organizing your work load that you are aware of deadlines as well as any time differences for other countries. Plan your work based both on priority and how long you take to complete a task. If an important project has to be completed in a week's time and you are confident of completing smaller projects in a few hours' time, it is better to complete the smaller project and then concentrate on the larger project once the first one is completed.

There are also outside constraints that may affect when you should begin working on certain projects. For example, you may have to work closely with another entity based in a country that is several hours ahead of you. Or, you may have to use a shipping company that has business hours different than your own. Be aware of people and time constraints so you can plan accordingly to maximize your time.

Delegate

As mentioned in Chapter Eleven, your employees are a significantly valuable resource when it comes to customer service. But, your employees are valuable also because of their expertise in various departments of your business. Make sure you utilize them to the best of their ability and that your management team is well versed in delegating appropriately. If an employee has spare time then they have time to take on other projects. Learn to delegate these projects so everyone's time is used efficiently and fully.

The Work Environment

Make sure you run an office that is conducive to working. If the environment is too staid, employees may not feel comfortable and work more carefully. While carefully working is not always a bad thing it can also mean slower productivity. However, if the environment is too casual, employees may feel lazy and not have a sense of urgency when meeting deadlines. Make it a point to remove all distractions like the television, coffee machines and magazine racks from the general work space and leave them for a break room or area.

The trick is to find a good balance between allowing your employees to feel comfortable and instilling a sense of urgency to ensure delivery is on time, every time.

Use Tools to Make your Job Easier

Use tools to help you streamline your processes. Make sure all software you use is standardized and available to each of your employees. Spend a little money investing in useful tools that will save time. Time is money after all and the small investment at the onset may very well save you a lot of money in the long run. You will find your company is running efficiently, allowing productivity to increase, and thus making your business more profitable.

If you are working with any type of manual process you will need to account for human error as well as an increased amount of time to complete. With the use of automated tools and software, though, you can alleviate some of these issues. You can decrease the amount of error with automated functions and you can accomplish jobs a lot easier.

Time Management Tools

There are many software programs for you to choose from to schedule your calendar for the day and week. You can create task lists and block time to accomplish particular goals and duties. Scheduling mechanisms such as those used in conjunction with your email are easy to use and quite handy. You can also build internal systems or consider online applications. Consider the needs of your entire company and determine a system that will fit everyone's needs.

Project Management Tools

There are many different project management software tools available that allow you to track every stage of a particular project. You can communicate both internally and externally as well as see any notes for the account all in one place. You can also pull data from the database to look at trends and anticipate needs. For example, you may find that in a particular month your sales double. You can be prepared for this rush ahead of time and take advantage of better pricing when you are aware of these trends.

The automated tools allow you to work more efficiently and allow you to save money. You can work smarter and benefit the bottom line. You won't be worried about spending more money in order to deliver on time. Instead, you will save money while exceeding your delivery expectations.

K.I.S.S.

K.I.S.S. is an acronym used commonly in business that means *"Keep it Simple, Silly"* or an alternative is *"Keep it Short and Simple"*.[5] Either one you prefer the basic premise is the same: **simplify, simplify, simplify.** If there is a way to streamline a process, this should be done. If there is a way to reduce paperwork, this should be done. In no case should there be duplication of efforts. If one employee or department already accomplishes a task for their purposes, this data should be available for others so they can avoid duplicating the task.

Remember to keep it as simple as possible. You want your processes to work quickly and efficiently. Plus, the easier a system is to use, the less time you have to take training others on how to use it. So, when evaluating any process for improvement, ask yourself if it is simple or overly complex.

Evaluate and Improve

Be aware of the time you take on each task throughout the day and week to see where there is room for improvement. Find out where there is wasted time or time that is not maximized for optimum efficiency. Evaluate the systems, software programs, policies and process you already have in place. Is it simple? Is there duplication? Are there any manual processes? Once you evaluate the systems, determine if there is a possibility for improvement in these areas.

Remember that even if you have to spend a little money to improve a system it will be well worth it in the long run and you will quickly recoup your investment with the added productivity and efficiency. All of this ultimately will help you deliver on time, every time without spending more money to do so.

CHAPTER THIRTEEN:

Establishing and Maintaining Relationships

Many of the chapters previously discussed in this book concentrate heavily on other people and other businesses that will help you achieve your own goals. These people and businesses are where you form relationships. Relationships are a necessary part of doing business and you have them with employees, vendors, partners, co workers, peers and clients. Every person you have to deal with in your operations has a relationship with you. How well you nurture and care for the relationship will directly affect how well you succeed in your business.

What is a Relationship?

In your personal life you do not question what a relationship is. You have a relationship with your family, your spouse or significant other, your children and your friends. But when it comes to business, not everyone considers the people they deal with on a daily basis as a relationship. However, it is imperative you think of it in these terms because just as the relationships in your personal life, your business relationships need to be cared for in order to be at their best.

Let's say you and your wife have been married for several years and have three children. Your wife is a home maker, taking care of the house and dealing with the children while you are at your job away from home. If you do not show your appreciation for the efforts she puts forth what will happen? If you ignore her and take her for granted, what will happen? Your wife will not be a happy person and you may suddenly find some things you took for granted lacking.

The same holds true in a business relationship but often on a much grander scale. You have relationships with everyone you come in contact with during your business dealings: internal and external relationships, peer to peer relationships, superior and subordinate relationships. Each one has its own dynamic and each one must be cared for. You can not ignore them. You can not take them for granted. You must show your appreciation. Respect is a key factor when it comes to nurturing these relationships.[1]

The Importance of Building Solid Business Relationships

When considering the importance if business relationships, look to the 80/20 rule which is considered valid. The 80/20 rule states that 80 percent of revenue comes from 20 percent of clients. Each client who produces towards the 80 percent is worth 16 times those who do not. Guy Kawasaki, one of the original Apple employees responsible for marketing the Macintosh, warns,

"Many companies waste millions of dollars trying to establish brands through advertising.... Brands are built on what people are saying about you, not what you are saying about yourself. People say good things about you when 1) you have a great product, and 2) you get people to spread the word about it."

And, even with the Internet's branding campaigns and other advanced marketing techniques, the most effective and efficient way to get people to spread the word is through a personal relationship and impeccable service.[2] Without relationships, there is no business, no product, no you.

One solid relationship can make you millions. Two and three can increase that exponentially to billions. More than that? You do the math. When you build one strong relationship it will have a ripple effect on all your other relationships. If one relationship is sound then that person or business entity will refer you to another. When you establish a positive business relationship with the first referral, that one will refer you to another and so on. Referrals are the most important tool a business has to expand their growth.

A two year research study compared actual customer behavior linked by questions to the consumer. The prevailing question that showed a positive impact on the company was, "Would you recommend this business to a friend?" This covered various types of industries. There was a direct correlation between the willingness of a customer to refer the company and the growth rate of the company. The more willing the customers were to refer to a friend or colleague, the more successful the business. This proves that referrals are incredibly important in business and establishing positive business relationships is tantamount in encouraging them.3 Positive business relationships are the number one indicator of customer loyalty. This is because it not only infers that the business produced a quality product at a fair price but that the customer is willing to put their own reputation on the line in order to recommend it.

"Do what you do so well that they will want to see it again and bring their friends."
— Walt Disney[4]

Choose Relationships Wisely

In your personal life you choose your relationships wisely. You do not have a relationship with just anyone who comes along because some relationships are toxic. They are not good for you and can force you to expend more energy than it is worth. Some relationships require a lot of work to maintain it with little to no return on your end. The same holds true with business relationships. You are investing a lot of time and energy to build and maintain these relationships and you must have a good return on your investment.

Do not put all your eggs in one basket. While you may have a particular client or vendor who is particularly beneficial to you, if it is the only one you have, you take on some risk. If that relationship does not work out for some reason (even if it is beyond your control) you are left scrambling to replace it. Instead, find different groups of companies to form strong relationships. That's how you will survive in the global market.

You have the potential to find business relationships wherever you go:

- *Via customer referrals*
- *While traveling*
- *Networking with industry groups*
- *Through sales leads*
- *By giving positive customer service to customers*
- *By dealing fairly with vendors*

But in order to make the most of these relationships you need to choose them wisely especially when you are dealing with partners, vendors and employees. There are even some customers that may be too taxing to take on. Instead, find a way to screen relationships so you surround yourself with positive ones and avoid the negative. If not, you will waste a lot of time and in some cases money.

Partners and Vendors

Choosing partners or vendors who positively impact your business is essential. Look for those who reciprocate fully in your relationship. You are dealing fairly with them. You are working with integrity, honesty, directness. Are they doing the same for you? Before choosing a relationship with a partner or vendor investigate them thoroughly. Look for testimonials. Check third party websites and get referrals. Make sure the partners and vendors you are establishing relationships with have a sound reputation for dealing fairly and honestly.

Make sure you also have more than one partner or vendor for each category. Do not put all your eggs in one basket so to speak. If you can diversify you have the ability to get more competitive pricing and are liable to have the ability to increase your business when you use multiple vendors. Plus, if the vendor goes out of business or has a difficult time and can not accommodate your needs either temporarily or when you grow, you have a backup that you can use without dealing with any delays in productivity.

Employees and Staff

As mentioned previously in Chapter Eleven: The Importance of Customer Service, employees are the backbone of your company. They too are in a relationship with you. From you they expect to be treated fairly, to have a positive work environment and earn a fair wage. In return you expect a positive work ethic, loyalty and competence. It is a symbiotic relationship that works like a finely tuned machine when all is well.

However, if things are not going well, if one party is not holding up their end of the relationship, employees have the potential to sorely damage your business and reputation. So, it is incredibly important to screen your potential candidates for a position carefully. Make sure they are the best for the job and evaluate them throughout their history with you. Nurture the relationship by training them and giving them responsibilities that allow them to grow as people and within your organization. Reward their efforts. If you do this, you will get back a great employee who is loyal and will go the extra mile.

Customers

Screen potential customers and groups of customers so that you have a solid base that is lucrative to your company. Find the clients that have money and who have the ability to buy your product. It is important to know who your good clients are. These are the customers who are low maintenance. They know what they want and do not use your resources to the extreme. Good clients need to be nurtured. Make sure you always make them aware their business is important to you and that you are there to help them if needed.

In order to determine the clients who should be nurtured the most, analyze your finances and identify the most profitable clients. This does not necessarily mean the clients who generate the most income. If a client spends $1,000 with your company but uses $500 in resources in order to close the deal is not nearly as ideal as a customer who only spends $800 but uses only $100 in resources. In the first scenario, you made a $500 profit but in the second you made $700 even though the first actually spent more money.

Now, do not get rid of clients just because they need a little more effort or work. But you do need to identify the times when doing so is beneficial to your business. You must know when to say no. In good times, dealing with bad clients can be an irritant but when times are bad, it can be devastating. Resources that are already stretched thin can not afford to be taken up by difficult clients and clients who are not profitable. But be careful that you act only on solid patterns. Every client or customer has the potential to have a "bad" time, a more difficult project or might need more hand holding than normal. Look at trends through a period of time as opposed to one off situations.

How to Develop Relationships

You need to work on your relationships and deal with each one in a positive manner. Respect, integrity, honesty and directness are all traits that should be present when dealing with your relationship. You need to look out for both your own interests as well as those of the person with whom you are dealing.

- *Communicate effectively and clearly.* If you can not explain your needs in a manner that is easily understood you may not get what you want. Be aware that not everyone communicates in the same manner so make sure you keep the lines open for a positive exchange.

- *Go the extra mile.* Do what you can to cater to your relationships. If you go the extra mile, chances are the other party in the relationship will reciprocate when you need it.

- *Be honest in your dealings with people.* Go the extra mile whenever you can, but be realistic. If you can not do something, be honest about it. Do not give false hope which will only back fire. Credibility will instill trust and trust will allow the other person to recommend you.

- *Be fair.* Just because you can get away with doing something that is not quite fair does not mean you should. Eventually this will be recognized if not done immediately. This will cause resentment and will sour the relationship.

- *Do what you say.* Be on time, show up when you say you will, and deliver what you promise. This will go a long way toward establishing trust and credibility within a relationship.[5]

• *Make sure the relationship is mutually beneficial.* Both parties need to give and get something out of the relationship. It does not have to be equal with every single transaction but over the course of time you should have the confidence and trust that the relationship you are in is an overall equitable one.

CONCLUSION

GOING GLOBAL.

It is obvious that going global in today's business environment makes sense. The United States makes up only a fraction of the population and thus the world's consumers. If you have a United States based business then you are limiting yourself by only catering to the local population. However, if you expand your business into other areas of the world you expose your product to millions, even billions more people. This means you can increase your customer base exponentially.

While the process behind expanding into a global marketplace may seem daunting, the information provided in this book will make the critical tasks a lot easier. The step-by-step instructions, resource materials and valuable advice will put you well on your way to planning and implementing a solid global business plan.

You have all the tools available to you to get you started with your business. Regardless of whether you are selling goods, services or projects, you too can find a market for it outside the United States and expand the number of potential customers you have.

Just remember:

- *Research your market*
- *Know the exporting regulations for your product*
- *Be familiar with the culture and environment of the foreign country*
- *Utilize quality support companies*
- *Find a trustworthy agent*
- *Establish an office in the foreign country when possible*
- *Take advantage of incentives*
- *Obtain tax breaks*
- *Use trade financing*
- *Travel*

- *Provide excellent customer service*
- *Deliver on time and*
- *Build and maintain solid relationships*

If you simply follow the advice as shown in this book, you too can successfully embark on an international business. You can set up and run a new business or take your existing company to a new level by expanding globally.

I sincerely hope my expertise and experience will help you in your endeavors. If you have any additional questions or want more information, please refer to my website at ***www.vernondarko.com***.

Vernon Darko

APPENDIX I: Interesting Facts

The following information is a collection of interesting facts that will allow you to see how the United States compares to other countries and continents in the world.

The World's Demographics

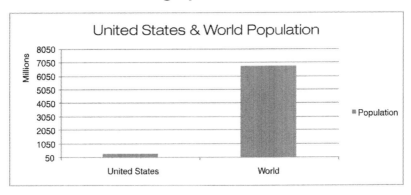

As of October 2009 the United States has over 300 million people with one birth every 7 seconds, one death every 13 seconds and one international migrant every 37 seconds for a net gain of one person every eleven seconds.[1]

The United States has over 3.5 million square miles and is the third largest country in the world with the third largest population.[2]

Over eighty percent of the population speaks English as the primary language.[2]

North America

North America consists of the United States, Mexico, Canada, Greenland, Saint Pierre, Miquelon and Bermuda.

As of October 2009 Canada has over 33 million people and based on growth statistics there is a net gain of one person every minute and 21 seconds.[3]

Canada has both English and French as their official language and it is a requirement to speak one or both to become a citizen.[4]

As of July 2009 Mexico has 111 million people with over 90 percent of the population speaking only Spanish.[5]

South America

South America consists of thirteen countries and one dependency for an overall population of over 380 million as of 2008.

The entire continent covers nearly 7 million square miles. It is the fourth largest continent and fifth in terms of population.

Spanish, English, French and Dutch are spoken throughout the continent with Spanish being the prevalent language across the land.[6]

Asia

There are nearly 60 countries throughout Asia with nearly 40 different languages spoken throughout the continent.[7]

As of 2008 Asia has over 4 billion people and accounts for over 60 percent of the world's population. It is first in both area and population.[8]

Africa

Africa is comprised of over sixty countries and territories. It is the second largest continent in terms of both area and population and over ten languages are prevalent throughout the region.[9]

Current estimates put the population of Africa right at one billion people. Africa is one of the fastest growing continents in terms of population and this growth has been seen in the last forty years making Africa a relatively young continent but a fast growing one.[10]

Europe

Europe is comprised of fifty sovereign states, seven non sovereign states, four partially recognized republics, territories and regions and two unrecognized republics, territories and regions.[11]

Current estimates put the 2010 population of Europe at over 728 million people but the population rate of growth seems to be slowing down significantly.[12]

English is spoken by many throughout Europe but there are many others broken down by Indo-European languages (Slavic, Germanic, Romance, Greek, Armenian, Albanian, Baltic, Indo-Iranian, Celtic), Semitic languages, Finno-Ugric languages, Altaic, Caucasian and Basque languages.[13]

Europe is nearly four million square miles and makes up nearly seven percent of the earth's land mass. It is the sixth largest continent as far as mass and third in population.[14]

Australia

Australia has nearly 22 million people as of March 2009, showing a 2 percent increase over the previous year.[15]

There is no official language but English is the language that is most prevalent throughout the country.[16]

The continent is nearly 3 million square miles.

Export Statistics

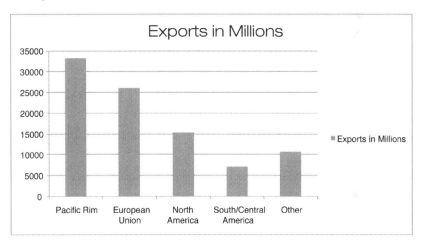

- The Department of Commerce via the U.S. Census Bureau gathers statistical analyses regarding the importing and exporting of goods and services. When considering going global, it is interesting to note some of these statistics as reported in the April 2008 report:17

- The United States imports $60.9 billion more than it exports currently.

- Exportation of good increased by $2.2 billion and services by $0.4 billion from March to April 2008.

• In 2008 there were approximately $430 billion in exports of goods. The largest of these categories was capital goods that include items such as computers, electronics, telecommunications equipment, business machines, semi conductors, drilling apparatus and civilian aircraft. Industrial supplies and materials was the next largest contributor followed by consumer goods, automotive vehicles, parts and engines, foods, feeds and beverages and finally "other" goods that are not otherwise categorized.

• The United States exported over $90 billion in 2008, the majority of which went to Pacific Rim countries such as China, Japan, Australia, Indonesia, Malaysia and the Philippines.

• The second most prevalent importer of U.S. exports is the European Union including France, Germany, Ireland, Italy and the UK.

APPENDIX II:
Helpful Organizations, Reference Materials and Websites

The following is a list of helpful materials. Some are used in citations throughout the book and some are useful sites or resources for additional research or inspiration. I highly recommend looking into these before starting your global enterprise:

Reference Materials

Babylon 8 (http://www.babylon.com/) – A subscription translation software package that will allow you to translate texts in multiple languages. This is not as good as human translation but better than most free sites.

Cultures and Organizations: Software of the Mind by Gert Jan Hofstede and Geert Hofstede

Delivering Knock Your Socks Off Service by Kristen Anderson

The Power of Positive Thinking by Norman Vincent Peale – ()

Rosetta Stone (http://www.rosettastone.com/) – The world's leading language tutorial. This is used by government agencies and schools to assist with learning a foreign language.

Your Best Life Now by Joel Osteen – (http://www.JoelOsteen.com)

Websites

Babelfish (http://babelfish.yahoo.com/) – This is a simple translation tool that can help with basic phrases but is not recommended for in depth communication.

Bankscope (bankscope2.bvdep.com) – A comprehensive, global database containing information on public and private banks.

Bureau of Industry and Security (http://www.bis.doc.gov) – Advances U.S. national security, foreign policy, and economic objectives by ensuring an effective export control and treaty compliance system and promoting continued U.S. strategic technology leadership.

Bureau Veritas (http://www.bureauveritas.com) – Delivers a comprehensive range of services including inspection, testing, auditing, certification, ship classification and related technical assistance, training and outsourcing. When appropriate, Bureau Veritas also provides advisory services.

U.S. Census Bureau (http://www.census.gov/) – Serves as the leading source of quality data about the nation's people and economy.

Central Intelligence Agency World Fact Book
(https://www.cia.gov/library/publications/the-world-factbook/geos/mx.html) – Gives general information on various countries.

U.S. Department of State Embassy Listings
(http://www.usembassy.gov/) – This site lists the embassies around the world.

Embassy World (http://embassyworld.com/) – Embassy World is designed to provide a comprehensive list of contact resources for all of the world's diplomatic offices.

Export.gov (http://www.export.gov/) – This site brings together resources from across the U.S. Government to assist American businesses in planning their international sales strategies and succeed in today's global marketplace.

Fitch Ratings (http://www.fitchratings.com) – A global rating agency committed to providing the world's credit markets with independent and prospective credit opinions, research, and data.

Moodys.com (http://moodys.com) – One of the world's most respected and widely utilized sources for credit ratings, research and risk analysis.

Wikipedia, the Free Encyclopedia (http://en.wikipedia.org) – This is a great resource for research on a variety of different topics. However, these are user submitted citations so it is best to have a secondary source to verify any information.

Organizations

Cotecna Inspection (http://www.cotecna.com) – One of the world's leading trade inspection, security and certification companies.

    58, rue de la Terrassière

    P.O. Box 6155

    1211 Geneva 6

    +41 22 849 6900

Export-Import Bank of the United States (http://www.exim.gov) – To assist in financing the export of U.S. goods and services to international markets.

    811 Vermont Avenue, N.W.

    Washington, DC 20571

    (202) 565-3946

U.S. Department of State (http://www.state.gov) – Provides a variety of information regarding foreign affairs.

    2201 C Street NW

    Washington, DC 20520

    (202) 647-4000

International Chamber of Commerce (http://www.iccwbo.org) – The voice of world business championing the global economy as a force for economic growth, job creation and prosperity.

    38 cours Albert 1er

    75008 Paris, France

    +33 1 49 53 28 28

International Finance Corporation (http://www.ifc.org) – This organization fosters sustainable economic growth in developing countries by financing private sector investment, mobilizing capital in the international financial markets, and providing advisory services to businesses and governments.

2121 Pennsylvania Avenue, NW
Washington, DC 20433 USA
(202) 473-1000

International Trade Administration (http://www.trade.gov/index.asp) – This site provides you access to ITA's valuable information and services regarding U.S. international trade policy.

1401 Constitution Ave NW
Washington, DC 20230
(800) USA TRAD(E)

The Office of Foreign Assets Control ("OFAC") of the US Department of the Treasury (http://www.treas.gov/offices/enforcement/ofac/) –This administers and enforces economic and trade sanctions based on US foreign policy and national security goals against targeted foreign countries and regimes, terrorists, international narcotics traffickers, those engaged in activities related to the proliferation of weapons of mass destruction, and other threats to the national security, foreign policy or economy of the United States.

1500 Pennsylvania Avenue, NW
Washington, D.C. 20220
(202) 622-2000

Piers Global Intelligence Solutions (http://www.piers.com) - A world leader in providing current, accurate and comprehensive data on international trade.

33 Washington Street

13th Floor

Newark, NJ 07102-3107

(973) 848-7051

SGS in The U.S.A. (http://www.us.sgs.com) – An organization that inspects, tests, verifies and certifies products exported from the U.S.

201 Route 17 North

Rutherford, NJ 07070

(201) 508 3000

APPENDIX III:

Definitions

The following is a list of definitions for easy reference throughout this book and in your global endeavors:

Agent – One who is authorized to act for or in the place of another; representative

Bill of Lading – A document issued by a carrier that lists goods being shipped and specifies the terms of their transport

Certificate of Origin – An official document listing the country and area from which a particular shipment started.

Commodity – An economic good, a product of agriculture or mining, an article of commerce especially when delivered for shipment, a mass-produced unspecialized product, something useful or valued

Competition – Two or more parties acting independently to secure the business of a third party by offering the most favorable terms

Consulting Company – An organization providing services such as data gathering in order to assist the growth of another company

Consumer – One who utilizes economic goods

Customer – One who purchases a commodity or service

Customs – Duties, tolls, or imposts imposed by the sovereign law of a country on imports or exports

Documentation Specialist – A person or organization that ensures all shipping and export documents are in order to ease the entrance into a foreign country

Export – To carry or send away a commodity or service to another country

Export License – An official document granting permission to remove a particular type of good from the country to ship to another

Freight Forwarding Company – A firm specializing in arranging storage and shipping of merchandise on behalf of its shippers

Global Marketplace – The mass of consumers who reside around the world and are not limited to the country of origin

Goods – A consignment of merchandise

Harmonized System (HS) – An internationally standardized system of names and numbers for classifying traded products developed and maintained by the World Customs Organization (WCO)

Import – To bring from a foreign or external source, to bring (as merchandise) into a place or country from another country

Inspections – To examine merchandise officially and carefully for allowance into the country

Letter of Credit – A letter addressed by a banker to a person to whom credit is given authorizing drafts on the issuing bank or on a bank in the person's country up to a certain sum and guaranteeing to accept the drafts if duly made

Manufacturing – to make into a product suitable for use, to make from raw materials by hand or by machinery, to produce according to an organized plan and with division of labor

Market Saturation – the supplying of a market with as much of a product as it will absorb

Networking - The exchange of information or services among individuals, groups, or institutions; specifically the cultivation of productive relationships for employment or business

North American Industry Classification System (NAICS) – Developed using a production-oriented conceptual framework, groups establishments into industries based on the activity in which they are primarily engaged. Establishments using similar raw material inputs, similar capital equipment, and similar labor are classified in the same industry.

Packing List – A list showing the number and kinds of items being shipped, as well as other information needed for transportation purposes

Partner – One associated with another especially in an action such as an associate or colleague

Prioritization – To list or rate such as projects or goals according to importance of completion

Product Classification – A means of grouping particular products such as by using the NAICS or HS for means of shipping and exporting

Projects – Combines both goods and services to accomplish a particular broad goal

Private Sector – That part of the economy which is both run for private profit and is not controlled by the state

Public Sector – The part of economic and administrative life that deals with the delivery of goods and services by and for the government

Schedule B – The document or form for Statistical Classification of Domestic and Foreign Commodities Exported from the United States

Services – Anything that does not require a tangible item or product

Supplier – someone whose business is to provide a particular service or commodity

Time Management – A range of skills, tools, and techniques used to manage time when accomplishing specific tasks, projects and goals to make the most of it

Trade Financing – Money lent to exporters or importers

Trade Incentives – Benefits to the importer or exporter to encourage business in a particular country, such as tax breaks, land discounts, etc.

Trade Party Screening – A group that is not allowed to accept goods or services from anyone exporting to that country. Exporters must know who can and cannot be traded with to remain complaint with exporting regulations.

Vendor – A business or person who sells a particular good or service

REFERENCES, CITATIONS AND END NOTES

The following is a list of all citations and notes that are used throughout this book. Each end note section is organized by chapter for convenience.

Chapter One

1"Product (business)." Wikipedia, The Free Encyclopedia.
11 November 2009. 13 November 2009.
<http://en.wikipedia.org/w/index.php?title=Product_(business)&oldid=325217921>.

2"U.S. Commercial Services." Department of Commerce International Trade Commission. 13 November 2009. <http://www.trade.gov/cs/>.

3"Directory & Search Engine Of Every Nation's Embassies & Consulates." Embassy World. 13 November 2009. 13 November 2009. < http://embassyworld.com/>.

4" Websites of U.S. Embassies, Consulates, and Diplomatic Missions." U.S. Department of State. 13 November 2009.
<http://www.usembassy.gov/>.

5"ICC Worldwide, National Committees and Groups." International Chamber of Commerce, The World Business Organization. 13 November 2009. < http://www.iccwbo.org/>.

Chapter Two

1"Schedule B." U.S. Census Bureau Foreign Trade. 01 September 2009. 11 November 2009. <http://www.census.gov/foreign-trade/schedules/b/>.

2"Export Licenses." Export.Gov. 11 November 2009. <http://www.export.gov/regulation/eg_main_018219.asp>.

3"SGS in the U.S." SGS in the U.S. 11 November 2009. <http://www.us.sgs.com/>.

4"Bureau Veritas Group." Bureau Veritas Group. 11 November 2009. <http://www.bureauveritas.com/wps/wcm/connect/bv_com/Group>.

5"Cotecna." Cotecna. 11 November 2009. <http://www.cotecna.com/COM/EN/home.aspx>.

6"Lists to Check." Bureau of Industry and Security, U.S. Department of Commerce. 11 November 2009. < http://www.bis.doc.gov/compliancean-denforcement/liststocheck.htm>.

Chapter Three

1"U.S. Commercial Services." Department of Commerce International Trade Commission. 13 November 2009. <http://www.trade.gov/cs/>.

2"Translate a Block of Text." Yahoo! Babelfish. 13 November 2009. <http://babelfish.yahoo.com/>.

3"Babylon 8." Babylon Translation at a Click. 11 November 2009.
<http://www.babylon.com/>.

4"Transparent Language." Transparent Language. 11 November
2009. <http://www.transparent.com/>.

5"Rosetta Stone." Rosetta Stone. 11 November 2009.
<http://www.rosettastone.com/>.

6"Wikipedia." Wikipedia. 11 Novemver 2009. <http://wikipedia.org/>.

7Hofstede, Geert. Cultures and Organizations: Software of the Mind.
2nd ed. New York, NY: McGraw-Hill, 1997. 49-78. Print.

8"Craigslist." Craigslist. 11 November 2009.
<http://www.craigslist.org/about/sites>.

9"Office of Foreign Assets Control." United States Department of the
Treasury. 11 November 2009. < http://www.treas.gov/offices/enforcement/ofac/>.

10"Moody's." Moodys.com. 11 November 2009.
<http://moodys.com/cust/default.asp>.

11"Fitch Ratings." Fitchratings.com. 11 November 2009.
<http://www.fitchratings.com/index_fitchratings.cfm>.

12"Bank Scope World Banking Information Source." BankScope. 11
November 2009. <https://bankscope2.bvdep.com/version-2009115/Home.serv?prod-
uct=scope2006>.

13"About IFC: Member Countries." International Finance Corporation.
2009. IFC, Web. 13 November 2009.
<http://www.ifc.org/ifcext/about.nsf/Content/Member_Countries>.

Chapter Four

1"Finding a Manufacturer." Start Up Nation. 18 November 2009.
<http://www.startupnation.com/articles/1293/1/finding-manufacturer.asp>.

2Ken Peters. "How to Find the Best Shipping Company for your Needs." ArticleClick. 21 June 2007. 18 November 2009.
<http://www.articleclick.com/Article/How-to-Find-the-Best-Shipping-Company-for-your-Needs/914873>.

3Better Business Bureau. <http://www.bbb.org/>.

4R. Kayne. "What is Freight Forwarding?" Wise Geek. 13 October 2009. 18 November 2009.
<http://www.wisegeek.com/what-is-freight-forwarding.htm>.

5"Common Export Documents." Export.Gov. 18 November 2009.
<http://www.export.gov/logistics/eg_main_018121.asp#P10_641>.

6"Fact Sheet." Craigslist. 26 September 2009. 18 November 2009.
<http://www.craigslist.org/about/factsheet>.

Chapter Five

1 "Programs and Services." The Corporate Council on Africa. Africacncl.org, Web. 13 November 2009.
<http://www.africacncl.org/Programs/index.asp>.

2 For example: http://www.usembassy.gov/ has all of the United States' embassy, consulate and diplomatic missions around the world and contact information for each of them.

3 http://www.trade.gov/cs/ and related links.

4 http://www.exim.gov/ and related links

Chapter Six

1"How to Establish an Office in Armenia." Russian American Chamber. 19 November 2009. 19 November 2009. <http://www.russianamericanchamber.com/en/services/office/armenia.htm>.

2The Corporate Council on Africa 16 November 2009. <http://www.africacncl.org/>.

Chapter Seven

1 Export Import Bank of the United States. 19 November 2009. 19 November 2009. <http://www.exim.gov>.

2 Opic. 19 November 2009. <http://www.opic.gov/>.

3 The World Bank. 19 November 2009. <http://www.worldbank.org/>.

4 International Finance Corporation. 19 November 2009. <http://www.ifc.org/>.

Chapter Eight

1 "North American Free Trade Agreement (NAFTA)." United States Department of Agriculture Foreign Agricultural Service. 19 November 2009. <http://www.fas.usda.gov/itp/Policy/nafta/nafta.asp>.

2 African Growth and Opportunity Act. 19 November 2009. <http://www.agoa.gov/>.

Chapter Nine

1Export Import Bank of the United States. 19 November 2009. 19 November 2009. <http://www.exim.gov>.

Chapter Ten

1David Grossman. "15 money-saving tips for business travelers." USA Today. 10 July 2006. 18 November 2009.
<http://www.usatoday.com/travel/columnist/grossman/2006-07-09-grossman_x.htm>.

Chapter Eleven

1Adrian Miller. "Customer Service Tips and Techniques." Business Know-How. 17 November 2009.
<http://www.businessknowhow.com/marketing/cstips.htm>.

2"Quotes of Customer Service." Sulekha.com. 17 November 2009.
<http://pnshukla.sulekha.com/blog/post/2007/01/quotes-of-customer-service.htm>.

3"Favorite Customer Service Quotes." Customer Service Point. 17 November 2009.
<http://www.customerservicepoint.com/customer-service-quotes.html>.

4Liz Tahir. "10 Customer Service Tips: Customer Service that will Keep them Coming Back." About.Com. 17 November 2009.
<http://sbinfocanada.about.com/od/customerservice/a/custservtipslt.htm>.
5"Telephone Etiquette, Customer Service Begins Here." SIUC.Edu. 17 November 2009. <http://www.infotech.siu.edu/telecom/etiquette.pdf>.

6Paul McFedries. "Netspeak." Word Spy: The Word Lover's Guide to New Words. 12 December 2001. 17 November 2009.
<http://www.wordspy.com/words/netspeak.asp>.

Chapter Twelve

1"Quotes of Customer Service." Sulekha.com. 17 November 2009.
<http://pnshukla.sulekha.com/blog/post/2007/01/quotes-of-customer-service.htm>.

2Hope Wilbanks. "Keeping Deadlines - Is it Really That Important?"
HubPages. 18 November 2009.
<http://hubpages.com/hub/Keeping-DeadlinesIs-It-Really-That-Important>.

3"How to Follow Up with Customers." More Business.com. 02 March
2009. 18 November 2009. <http://www.morebusiness.com/customer-follow-up>.

4"Personal Time Management Guide." Time-management-Guide.com.
18 November 2009. <http://www.time-management-guide.com/>.

5"What Does KISS Stand For?" Acronym Finder. 18 November 2009.
<http://www.acronymfinder.com/KiSS.html>.

Chapter Thirteen

1"Business Relationships." Leading Insight. 19 November 2009.
<http://www.leadinginsight.com/business_relationships.htm>.

2Jonathan Yates. "The Importance of Building Relationships." All
Business.com. New Hampshire Business Review. 05 December 2008.
<http://www.allbusiness.com/company-activities-management/product-management-
branding/11736449-1.html>.

3 Frederick F. Reichheld. "One Number You Need to Grow." Harvard
Business. 01 December 2003. 19 November 2009.
<http://harvardbusiness.org/product/one-number-you-need-to-grow/an/R0312C-PDF-
ENG>.

4 "Quotes of Customer Service." Sulekha.com. 17 November 2009.
<http://pnshukla.sulekha.com/blog/post/2007/01/quotes-of-customer-service.htm>.

5 Ivan Misner. "Build Relationships That Last." Entrepreneur. 26 May 2003. 19 November 2009.
<http://www.entrepreneur.com/marketing/networking/article62140.html>.

Appendix One References

1"U.S. POPClock Projection." U.S. Census Bureau. 31 August 2009. 28 October 2009. <http://www.census.gov/population/www/popclockus.html>.

2"Profile of the People and Land of the United States." National Atlas. 17 September 2009. 28 October 2009.
<http://www.nationalatlas.gov/articles/mapping/a_general.html>.

3"Canada's Population Clock." Statistics Canada. 20 July 2009. 28 October 2009. <http://www.statcan.gc.ca/edu/clock-horloge/edu06f_0001-eng.htm>.

4"Learning English and French." Citizenship and Immigration Canada. 31 May 2009. 28 October 2009.
<http://www.cic.gc.ca/english/newcomers/before-language.asp>.

5"The World Fact Book." Central Intelligence Agency. 06 October 2009. 28 October 2009.
<https://www.cia.gov/library/publications/the-world-factbook/geos/mx.html>.

6"List of South American Countries and Territories." Wikipedia, The Free Encyclopedia. 26 October 2009. 28 October 2009.
<http://en.wikipedia.org/wiki/List_of_South_American_countries_and_territories>.

7"List of Asian Countries and Territories." Wikipedia, The Free Encyclopedia. 20 October 2009. 28 October 2009.

<http://en.wikipedia.org/w/index.php?title=List_of_Asian_countries_and_territories&oldid=3
21031546>.

8 "World population." Wikipedia, The Free Encyclopedia. 28 October
2009. 28 October 2009.
<http://en.wikipedia.org/w/index.php?title=World_population&oldid=322558124>.
9 "List of African Countries and Territories." Wikipedia, The Free
Encyclopedia. 28 October 2009. 28 October 2009.
<http://en.wikipedia.org/w/index.php?title=List_of_African_countries_and_territories&oldid=
322506294>.

10 "Africa: Continent's Population reaches One Billion." AllAfrica.Com.
20 August 2009 28 October 2009.
<http://allafrica.com/stories/200908200660.html>.

11"List of European countries." Wikipedia, The Free Encyclopedia. 27
October 2009. 28 October 2009.
<http://en.wikipedia.org/w/index.php?title=List_of_European_countries&oldid=322426188>.

12"Historic, Current and Future Population of Europe." GeoHive. 18
June 2008. 28 October 2009.
<http://www.geohive.com/earth/his_proj_europe.aspx>.

13"Languages of Europe." Wikipedia, The Free Encyclopedia. 22
October 2009. 28 October 2009.
<http://en.wikipedia.org/w/index.php?title=Languages_of_Europe&oldid=321356343>.

14"Europe." World Atlas. 28 October 2009.
<http://www.worldatlas.com/webimage/countrys/eu.htm>.

15"3101.0 - Australian Demographic Statistics, Mar 2009." Australian
Bureau of Statistics. 20 October 2009. 28 October 2009.
<http://www.abs.gov.au/ausstats/abs@.nsf/mf/3101.0>.

16"Australia." Wikipedia, The Free Encyclopedia. 28 October 2009. 28 October 2009.

<http://en.wikipedia.org/w/index.php?title=Australia&oldid=322527840>.

17"U.S. Census Bureau U.S. Bureau of Economic Analysis NEWS." U.S. Census Bureau. 10 June 2008. 28 October 2009.

<http://www.census.gov/foreign-trade/Press-Release/2008pr/04/ft900.pdf>.

Made in the USA
Middletown, DE
28 December 2017